MOTIVATIONAL ENNEAGRAM TYPE TEST

COMPREHENSIVE AND IN-DEPTH ENNEAGRAM TEST IN 100 QUESTIONS FROM 100 AREAS OF LIFE

DETLEF RATHMER

AF215919

9 **8** **1** **7** **2** **6** **3** **5** **4**

RECOGNIZE YOUR TRUE

MOTIVATION!

RECOGNIZE YOURSELF!

WHO ARE YOU?
WHAT DRIVES YOU IN LIFE?
FIND THE TRUE CORE OF YOUR PERSONALITY,
FIND YOUR TRUE ENNEAGRAM TYPE AND THEN
LIVE A CONSCIOUS AND FULFILLING LIFE!

1 ST EDITION JULY 2019

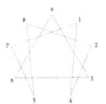

Bibliographic information of the German National Library

The German National Library lists this publication in the Deutsche Nationalbibliografie; detailed bibliographic data is available on the Internet at www.dnb.de.

Important note: Medicine as a science is constantly in flux. Research and experience expand our knowledge, especially regarding treatment and drug therapy. Insofar as a dosage or application is mentioned in this work, the reader may trust that authors, editors and publishers have taken great care to ensure that this information corresponds exactly to the level of knowledge at the time the work is completed. However, each user is encouraged to review the package leaflets of the products used to determine if the recommendation for dosages given or the contraindication given there differs from what is stated in this book. This applies not only to preparations that are rarely used or newly placed on the market, but also to those that have been restricted in their applicability by the Federal Health Office (BGA) or Paul-Ehrlich Institut (PEI). Protected trademarks (trademarks) are not specially marked. From the absence of such a note it cannot be concluded that it is a free trade name.

www.verlagshaus-rathmer.com

QR-Code Publishing House Rathmer:

Production and publishing: BoD- Books on Demand, Norderstedt

© (Copyright) Detlef Rathmer

ISBN: 9783749470082

Editing: Giuseppina ("Pina") Grozotis, Jonah S. Rathmer, Detlef Rathmer

Creative support: David L. Rathmer

Technical support: Jonah S. Rathmer

Homepage Publishing House Rathmer: www.verlagshaus-rathmer.com

Detlef Rathmer
Molkereiweg 9
48727 Billerbeck
Tel.: (+49) (0)2543/931 85 07
Email: 9Rathmer@gmail.com
www.verlagshaus-rathmer.com

1. Introduction

With the **Motivational Enneagram Type Test** you are able to determine your Enneagram type safely and reliably. In the practice of typing to take such a test, one of the main obstacles encountered is often unnoticed by many test users, and this is due to: *The perceiving subjective consciousness of each person has a a more or less distorted view of the world!* As human beings, without exception, we are subject to a certain subjectivity, and every human being, due to his **so-called blind spot** and because of the *individual`s psychological make-up* looks unconsciously *through the lens of his/her own Enneagram Type,* which may cause his or her own perception to distort, discolor, or change. However, this variable blurriness for each human being and test user can be minimized as much as possible by a *variety of very different questions from all areas of life,* as you will find here in this type test with a total of **100 test questions**.

In this way, this **Motivational Enneagram Type Test** provides you, so to speak, with *one of the most important keys to self-knowledge about your Enneagram type* and at the same time your *true motivation as a human being.* The *second key to understanding your own Enneatype* is MINDFULLNESS. Mindfulness understood in this test is the key to most reliable test results. Therefore, be very honest in answering the 100 test questions of this Enneagram test, try to gather as consciously as possible in the so-called here-and-now to answer the questions conscientiously and accurately, to the best of your knowledge and belief. If possible be truly yourself. Take your time, there is absolutely no advantage in rushing this stage. Remember: The path is the destination, i.e. every single step on the way to the end result is much more important than the goal itself. So make sure you take your test in a room which is free from interference before you start taking the test. The goal is not to complete the test in record time. Only then you will be able to arrive at a reliable and objective test result.

Another helpful strategy to take a conscious deep breath before each question and open yourself inwardly as attentively and undisturbed as possible for the upcoming question. Take a deep breath - exhale for a long time and relax as much as possible when exhaling, because the next inhalation will certainly come anyway without your own effort. It's best to focus your attention on the breathing process itself. From this state, you begin to get an understanding of each of the individual questions, and that's enough to get a good, useful, and above all, reliable test result. Some questions will be easier, some harder to answer - in the latter case ask familiar people for help.

This carefully designed type test is called **"motivational"**, so it is fundamentally based on *human **motivation***. For a more reliable indication of the Enneatype it is absolutely necessary to determine the ***true essential basic motivation*** of a person. In addition, one can use the *purely psychological action and behavioral patterns* of a person only conditionally, but it is more important to determine what is underlying the action; that is, the so-called intrinsic motivation. For this reason, in Enneagram circles the saying goes: *The behavior is nothing - the motivation is EVERYTHING!* Most of the Enneagram type tests, however, are primarily based on focusing on the behavior of a person to be typed, so that false typing will always occur. In contrast, in this **Motivational Enneagram Type Test**, the focus of the 100 test questions is on the underlying motivational basic structures of personality, i.e. on the "why" of the specific behavioral and action patterns of humans. This makes it a reliable type test for determining one`s own Enneatype!

So, if an Enneagram test can claim to be reliable then it certainly is a motivational type test because it takes into account the deeper motivations of a person. Nevertheless, one should not rely blindly on the test result, because such a test can never be „perfect". Therefore, the test result should always be seen under reserve. On the other hand, the result of this Enneagram type test can quite reliably provide the reader with a way to somehow separate the wheat from the chaff to subsequently confirm the result by further self-recognition processes. The reliability of the test result, as described in detail above, is directly and closely related to one's own ability to objectively self-reflect and exercise "self-honesty". Regrettably, every person, even the most self-aware, has more or less the well-known "blind spot". In any case, we should always be aware of this when performing this test, as this awareness will lead to more accurate, more reliable test results.

So if you want the end result of your test to be reliable *(see chapter 5 on page 69)*, then please have the courage to be as honest as possible to yourself!

Detlef Rathmer in July 2019

2. Contents

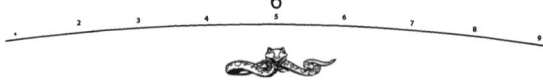

Avoidance Strategies of the 9 Enneatypes, their Drives * and Main Passions (inner cirle)

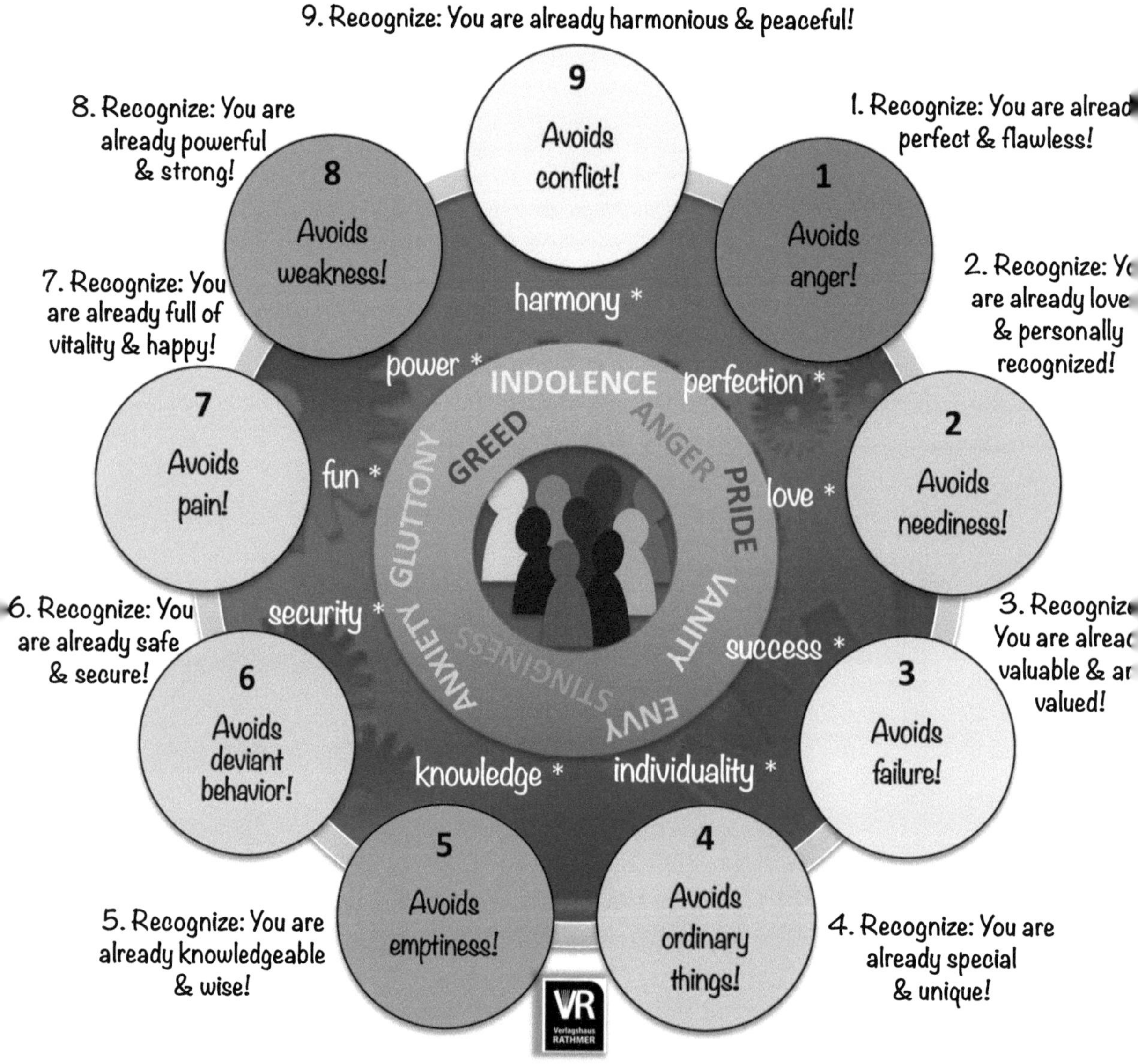

9. Recognize: You are already harmonious & peaceful!

8. Recognize: You are already powerful & strong!

1. Recognize: You are alread[y] perfect & flawless!

7. Recognize: You are already full of vitality & happy!

2. Recognize: Y[ou] are already love[d] & personally recognized!

6. Recognize: You are already safe & secure!

3. Recogniz[e] You are alread[y] valuable & ar[e] valued!

5. Recognize: You are already knowledgeable & wise!

4. Recognize: You are already special & unique!

9 Avoids conflict!

8 Avoids weakness!

1 Avoids anger!

7 Avoids pain!

2 Avoids neediness!

6 Avoids deviant behavior!

3 Avoids failure!

5 Avoids emptiness!

4 Avoids ordinary things!

harmony *
power *
perfection *
fun *
love *
security *
success *
knowledge *
individuality *

INDOLENCE
GREED
ANGER
PRIDE
VANITY
STINGINESS
ENVY
ANXIETY
GLUTTONY

VR
Verlagshaus
RATHMER

* These drives represent *the true motivations of a person*, according to which he behaves automatically, which he is not aware of. The particular enneatype attempts to satisfy a deficiency that is hidden deep inside, which often succeeds in the short term. In reality, however, the effect of this life strategy does not last long, and only **self-knowledge about one's enneatype** and its true impulse, and the prescription of the most appropriate homeopathic enneagram remedy, can lead to **liberation through awareness**.

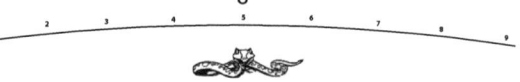

4. Motivational Enneagram Type Test in 100 questions
(from 100 areas of life)

Please rate the following, alphabetically ordered **100 areas of life** according to the **two most relevant main motives** by marking the **two most important** (*1 = very important, 2 = the second most important*) of the **9 statements** of the 100 test questions with the **numbers 1** and **2**:

TOPIC	ACCIDENT REACTIONS	1 = very important
Question 1	On the occasion of an accident, I mainly react in two of the following ways (reactions to an accident):	2 = second important
S	I recognize the terrible dimension of the situation and do everything I can to maintain order and alert the emergency service.	
Y	I recognize the factual dimension and log the exact accident details according to the facts.	
X	I recognize the pragmatic dimension and provide action-oriented support/help.	
O	I recognize the ethical dimension of the situation, ask who is responsible and collect information.	
Z	I recognize the urgency, the extent of the situation and look for ways to improve it.	
F	I recognize the emotional dimension of the shock/emotional overload and calm the participants.	
T	I recognize the human dimension of the situation and wonder if anything has happened to the people involved and how I can help.	
N	I recognize the confusing dimension of the situation and am available for everything that is needed.	
E	I recognize the need to take leadership and responsibility for the situation and provide first aid.	

TOPIC	ANIMAL EQUIVALENTS	1 = very important
Question 2	With which two enumerations of the following do I personally and spontaneously identify with?	2 = second important
O	Ant, crane, vulture, goose, bee, billy goat, terrier, mouse.	
Y	Hedgehog, badger, fox, owl, starfish, mole, hamster, parrot.	
N	Whale, bear, turtle, koala, elephant, lamb, sloth, dolphin.	
F	Penguin, basset hound, frog, baby seal, nightingale, pug, duckling.	
E	Bull, lion, hippopotamus, shark, rhinoceros, bulldog, tiger, crocodile.	
X	Chameleon, poodle, kingfisher, ornamental fish, tomcat, toucan, peacock, hummingbird.	
Z	Monkey, zebra, cow, giraffe, butterfly, otter, guinea pig, crow.	
T	Cat, donkey, pig, kangaroo, panda, seahorse, swan, hen.	
S	Snail, mouse, deer, rabbit, hare, German shepherd dog, panther, wolf.	

TOPIC	ATTENTION IN RELATIONSHIPS	1 = very important
Question 3	In interpersonal relationships, my attention is particularly focused on the following two points:	2 = second important
X	Recognition in terms of tasks and achievements.	
T	Recognition for one`s own person.	
E	Control of relationship partners.	
S	The hidden intentions of others.	
N	The attitude of others.	
O	The question: What is right or wrong about or in the situation?	
F	The best in the absent, the worst in the existing.	
Z	Pleasant alternatives.	
Y	The question: What does the other want from me? Privacy?	

TOPIC	ATTITUDE TOWARDS PARENTS	1 = very important
Question 4	Which two psychic attitudes of the following nine do I most likely possess with regard to my parents?	2 = second important
X	Positive attitude towards the mother - connectedness / gratitude.	
O	Negative attitude towards the father - separateness.	
S	Positive attitude towards the father - connectedness / gratitude.	
E	Ambivalence towards the mother - ambiguity.	
F	Negative attitude towards both parents - separateness.	
N	Positive attitude towards both parents - connectedness / gratitude.	
T	Ambivalence towards the father - ambiguity.	
Y	Ambivalence towards both parents - ambiguity.	
Z	Negative attitude towards the mother - separateness.	

TOPIC	AVOIDANCE STRATEGIES	1 = very important
Question 5	The following two avoidance strategies are particularly and personally familiar to me:	2 = second important
Y	I avoid emptiness/emotional closeness and search for knowledge!	
S	I avoid deviant behavior and search for security!	
F	I avoid the ordinary/feeling lost and looking for individuality!	
X	I avoid failure and search for success!	
Z	I avoid pain and search for enjoyment of life and fun!	
E	I avoid weakness and seek control and power!	
T	I avoid neediness and search for love and being loved!	
N	I avoid conflicts/confrontations and search for harmony!	
O	I avoid anger and search for perfection!	

TOPIC	BASIC FEARS	1 = very important
Question 6	**Which two basic fears, other concerns and uncertainties are particularly anchored in me?**	2 = second important
N	Separation, segregation, divorce in any form, conflict.	
Y	Incomprehensibility, of being overwhelmed, of losing everything, of emotional opening.	
S	Fear of betrayal, being exposed, insecurity.	
F	From own inadequacy, from being abandoned, from having a deficiency.	
Z	From boredom, exertion, deprivation, pain & suffering.	
E	Of being defeated, injured, weak and dependent.	
T	To be unloved, to be rejected (by emotional refusal).	
X	To be meaningless or worthless, from failure, defeat.	
O	To be condemned, for not being good enough, to make a mistake.	

TOPIC	BEHAVIOR TOWARDS ONE´S OWN CHILDREN	1 = very important
Question 7	**The behaviour towards my children is especially characterized by two of the following descriptions:**	2 = second important
F	I recognize and support the creative potential of the children and their feelings, either overcritical or too lax.	
N	I am helpful, kind, warm-hearted, let too much pass, do not give instructions, peaceful, tend to be anti-authoritarian.	
O	I teach a lot of responsibility and moral values to the children, I'm consistent and fair, I practice strict discipline.	
T	I listen well to the children, I am warm-hearted, encouraging, playful, self-critical about the "right" education, self-sacrificing.	
X	I am steady, loyal, reliable, torn between work and children, expecting order and responsibility from them.	

Continued question 7 see next page …

TOPIC	BEHAVIOR TOWARDS ONE´S OWN CHILDREN	1 = very important
Question 7	The behaviour towards my children is especially characterized by two of the following descriptions:	2 = second important
E	I am caring, loyal, devotional, I stand up for my children, sometimes overprotective, demanding, stubborn, constant monitoring of the children, too controlling.	
Z	I am generous, enthusiastic, want to offer exciting things to the children, do not tend to pay enough attention to them because of my own activities.	
S	I am loving, caring, I have a strong sense of duty, and I am reluctant to let the children enjoy their independence.	
Y	I am kind, empathetic, do everything for the children, sometimes authoritarian, demanding, expect high intellectual performances, intolerant of overly strong feelings.	

TOPIC	BEHAVIOR TOWARDS SOCIETY	1 = very important
Question 8	My social behavior towards society tends to express itself in the following two ways:	2 = second important
N	Most of the time I stay outside and don't really get involved with society. I close myself off and avoid problems/conflict.	
O	I always try to be a good person, a good member of society and I get angry about norm violations.	
Z	For me, my needs come first, and often it overwhelms me to meet the needs of others.	
X	I interpret and use the rules of society according to my advantage and for my purposes effectively and optimally.	
Y	I tend to reject society and prefer to act independently; rules and regulations annoy me.	
E	I'm always on guard, do not let anyone get too close to me. I can handle it all on my own, I don`t need company.	

Continued question 8 see next page …

… continued question 8:

TOPIC	BEHAVIOR TOWARDS SOCIETY	1 = very important
Question 8	My social behavior towards society tends to express itself in the following two ways:	2 = second important
T	I am interested in and take care of the needs of society, sometimes neglecting myself.	
F	I present myself as unapproachable to society and as something special, sometimes I seek society`s attention.	
S	I offer my help with restraint and make commitments without losing my independence.	

TOPIC	BELIEFS	1 = very important
Question 9	Which of the following two inner beliefs seem to me to be particularly familiar?	2 = second important
T	I'm not lovable and meaningless.	
O	There's something wrong with me, I have a major flaw.	
Z	I'm cut off from the source of life (of enjoyment).	
E	I'm weak, needy, bad and I have to fight all the time.	
S	I'm weak and incompetent, the world is hostile.	
Y	I'm empty and isolated inside.	
F	I have been abandoned and separated from everything.	
N	I'm unimportant and unlovable!	
X	I'm empty and insubstantial.	

TOPIC	BLINDNESS/BLIND SPOT	1 = very important
Question 10	Sometimes I have a limited perception of reality, a blindness/blind spot for:	2 = second important
Z	Needs of others, not recognizing own fears and pain.	
O	Emotional nuances/own irritability.	
E	Personal freedom of others / own vulnerability, need for attention.	
T	The dignity of others/own needs and feelings.	
Y	Personal needs of others/own physical condition, own feelings and needs.	
F	The good in the existing/own ordinariness, own good qualities.	
S	Personal motives of other/inner guidance and that other people offer help.	
X	Personal qualities of others/inner emptiness and self-denial.	
N	The essentials in a situation/own advantages and strengths.	

TOPIC	BOOK READING	1 = very important
Question 11	In my spare time, a good book should definitely meet the following two criteria:	2 = second important
Y	It has to provide new information.	
T	There must be some sort of life coaching.	
N	It should generate moments of happiness.	
F	It should have artistic claim, be sophisticated.	
S	It should be traditional with a historical background.	
Z	It should be fun to read.	
X	It should be promising.	
E	There should be a knowledge advantage over others.	
O	It should be challenging and educating.	

TOPIC	CAR PURCHASE	1 = very important
Question 12	The two most important reasons when buying a private car are for me:	2 = second important
N	Inconspicuous, comfortable.	
E	PS-strong car, with which you can overtake well.	
Z	Driving pleasure.	
S	Safety and security.	
Y	Economic efficiency, economy.	
F	Uniqueness, unusualness.	
X	Chic, sporty, impressive shape (image).	
T	Spaciousness (plenty of space for family and objects).	
O	Perfect technique and high quality workmanship.	

TOPIC	CAR TYPES	1 = very important
Question 13	Which two categories of car types do I personally prefer regardless of my current life situation?	2 = second important
Y	Oldtimer	
Z	Convertible	
S	Small car or SUV	
X	Sports car	
O	Limousine (elegant)	
E	Off-road vehicle with a lot of horsepower	
T	Camper	
F	Special model	
N	Combi (useful, practical)	

TOPIC	CENTRAL AREAS OF LIFE	1 = very important
Question 14	Which of the following two central areas of life have always been of great importance in my life?	2 = second important
N	health & harmony	
E	wealth & power	
Z	children & happiness	
S	family & safety	
Y	knowledge & collecting	
F	helpful friends & individuality	
X	career & success	
T	partnership & becoming loved	
O	fame & perfection	

TOPIC	CHALLENGES TO LIFE	1 = very important
Question 15	Which two living challenges do I face particularly intensively in my life?	2 = second important
O	To wrestle with all senses!	
S	To deal with all your senses!	
N	To love and to act with all senses!	
X	To shape with all senses!	
T	To search and find with all senses!	
F	To trust with all senses and to recognize yourself!	
Y	To strive for the truth with all senses!	
Z	To live with all senses!	
E	To believe with all senses!	

TOPIC	CHILDHOOD DEFICITS	1 = very important
Question 16	In my childhood two of the following childhood deficits (parental claims) prevailed to a special degree:	2 = second important
T	You can't have your own needs!	
S	You can`t think too much about yourself!	
E	You can't trust anyone or show your feelings!	
F	You can't want to be too perfect or too happy!	
N	You can`t always enforce your head!	
O	You can't make any mistakes!	
X	You can't have your own feelings and your own will!	
Z	You can't rely on others!	
Y	You can't make it too easy for yourself!	

TOPIC	COMIC FIGURES (ASTERIX & OBELIX)	1 = very important
Question 17	Which figures from "Asterix & Obelix" can I identify with in a special way/very well?	2 = second important
F	Troubadix (the bard, the opinions about his talent are divided).	
E	Automatix (blacksmith of the Gallic village, scrappy craftsman).	
X	Asterix (always has the best ideas, best friend of Obelix).	
S	Amnesix (druid with memory loss, expert on mental diseases).	
O	Julius Caesar (Roman emperor, occupied the whole of France and wanted to subjugate the indomitable, resistive Gauls).	
T	Gibtermine (receptionist & secretary, assigns appointments to patients).	
N	Obelix (menhir supplier & fallen into the magic potion as a child).	
Z	Gutemine (pragmatic wife of Chief Majestix).	
Y	Miraculix (the venerable druid of the village, magic potion maker).	

TOPIC	COMPETITION INCLINATION	1 = very important
Question 18	In my opinion, these are the two sports disciplines in which I would be most likely to achieve top performances:	2 = second important
T	rescue flying	
N	cross-country skiing	
F	gliding, sail flying	
Y	billiard	
E	boxing	
Z	dancing	
S	volleyball	
O	chess	
X	golfing	

TOPIC	CONCEPTS (ASPECTS, CHARACTERISTICS, FACTS)	1 = very important
Question 19	Which two main concepts do I personally recognize in my life and what do they lead to?	2 = second important
S	Concept of lack of courage leads to fear and self-doubt.	
N	Concept of inertia leads to a halt.	
O	Concept of perfectionism leads to anger.	
F	Concept of false lack leads to envy.	
O	Concept of false abundance leads to pride.	
E	Concept of anti-authoritarian life leads to rebellion.	
X	Concept of being seen leads to vanity.	
Y	Concept of not having enough leads to stinginess.	
Z	Concept of lack of liveliness leads to insatiability.	

TOPIC	CORE RESOURCES	1 = very important
Question 20	Which two characteristic core resources (lifeline) are very typical for me in case of problems?	2 = second important
E	self-assurance	
O	rational thinking	
Y	power of observation	
F	self-inquiry	
T	empathy	
Z	enjoyment of life	
X	orientation to other people	
S	relationship skills	
N	interest in people	

TOPIC	DEALING WITH ILLNESS	1 = very important
Question 21	Which two descriptions in dealing with disease/illness/symptoms apply most to me?	2 = second important
E	I don`t let the disease get me down, do everything to get strong and healthy again quickly.	
F	I become more hysterical because of my diagnosis and ask myself "why me?" and emphasize the suffering and the pain.	
Z	I often get severe symptoms, quickly resort to painkillers, aspirin etc., so that I soon feel well again.	
X	I would like to be operational again as soon as possible in order to be able to resume my work.	
S	I am afraid that the symptoms may worsen and desperately looking for solutions, I am careful and anxious.	
T	I seek personal conversation, comfort and encouragement, I am suspicious of the consequences of the therapy, but still open-hearted.	

Continued question 21 see next page …

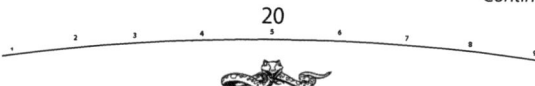

… continued question 21:

TOPIC	DEALING WITH ILLNESS	1 = very important
Question 21	**Which two descriptions in dealing with disease/illness/symptoms apply most to me?**	2 = second important
Y	Above all, I would like to know the cause and background of the disease in order to be able to explain it to myself.	
O	I only seek help when I myself no longer know what to do, I am critical and distanced with regard to the therapy.	
N	I like to put the responsibility into the hands of others, I behave rather passive-diffuse and sluggish towards the symptoms and also emphasize trivialities of the disease.	

TOPIC	DEFENSE MECHANISM	1 = very important
Question 22	**To be honest, the following two defense mechanisms are particularly familiar to me in relation to my person:**	2 = second important
Y	Isolation, retreat, analysis, encapsulation, segmentation, reduction - I reduce my feelings and impulses so much that they are no longer threatening.	
T	Repression, suppression - I perceive my feelings and impulses, but I suppress them more or less successfully.	
E	Denial, rejection, ignorance - I perceive my feelings and impulses, but I ignore them when they are disturbing.	
S	Projection - I project my feelings and impulses to the outside.	
X	Identification - I am completely identified with feelings and impulses.	
N	(Self)Numbness, compulsive thinking - I numb my feelings and impulses, which are therefore hardly or not at all accessible.	
Z	Rationalization - I use my mind and argue my feelings and impulses.	
F	Artificial sublimation, introjection - I raise and alienate my feelings and impulses in images and metaphors.	
O	Reaction control, unconscious reaction formation - I deny my feelings and impulses as if they did not exist.	

TOPIC	DEFICITS IN THE FAMILY OF ORIGIN	1 = very important
Question 23	When I think of my childhood and my family of origin, which two main aspects were there at that time?	2 = second important
Z	Limited perception, narrow perspective - attention deficit.	
X	No bond between the family members - pressure of expectations.	
S	Lack of security or support - parental incompetence.	
N	Lack of harmony and peace - invisible needlessness.	
Y	No guidance, no real understanding - intrusive upbringing.	
T	No love between the parents - own fight for love.	
O	Love was conditional, a barter, a trade - punishment reward.	
F	Lack of self-confidence - frequent loss of love.	
E	Conflicts or confusion regarding power - experience of violence.	

TOPIC	DIRECTIONS OF ATTENTION	1 = very important
Question 24	My attention is generally focused especially on the following two questions:	2 = second important
E	What endangers my control? What is vulnerable?	
X	What is efficient and successful?	
N	What is harmonious? What are your positions, opinions, wishes?	
T	What is needed? What needs do you have?	
O	What is wrong and needs to be corrected?	
F	What is missing for me existentially?	
S	What can be wrong, what bad intentions do I encounter?	
Y	What is observable? Which expectations overwhelm me?	
Z	What is feasible, possible, what nice alternatives are there?	

TOPIC	DRIVING STYLE	1 = very important
Question 25	**The following two driving styles are the most familiar and personal to me:**	2 = second important
T	Considerate, cooperative, yielding.	
S	Anxious-defensive, hesitant or intimidating, sure.	
Y	Thoughtful, observant, defensive-reserved.	
O	Fast-offensive, rule-compliant, distanced-critical.	
X	Fast-reacting, sporty-elegant, overtaking, focused.	
Z	Brash and cheerful, lively, friendly, fast.	
N	Slow-defensive, continuous, gentle-comfortable, on autopilot.	
E	Showing strength, dominant, controlling, often too fast.	
F	Elitist-conceited, sensitive-seeking, internalized-individual.	

TOPIC	EATING & DRINKING	1 = very important
Question 26	**In my diet, two things are especially important to me:**	2 = second important
N	Simple food, frugal, enough and it must taste good for everyone.	
F	Special, high quality, healthy, exclusive dishes.	
X	Exquisite, expensive meals that "represent something", rich table.	
S	Usual, proven dishes, not very adventurous, standard.	
O	Selected, healthy, nutritious, quality, cheap.	
Z	"Fingerfood", slow enjoyment, joy of eating, preference for sour.	
Y	Meager, frugal, spartan, put little value on food, cheap.	
E	Eating excessively, large portions, spicy, greasy, tends to be unhealthy.	
T	Home cooking, with love for others and me to cook and bake.	

TOPIC	EDUCATIONAL EXPERIENCES	1 = very important 2 = second important
Question 27	**Unfortunately, in my childhood I had to experience two of the following educational experiences in a painful way:**	
E	Violence experience!	
Y	Intrusive upbringing!	
T	Love fight!	
Z	Attention Deficit!	
S	Parental incompetence!	
X	Fulfillment of expectations!	
F	Loss of love!	
N	Invisible needlessness!	
O	Punishment - Reward!	

TOPIC	EGO PERSONALITY	1 = very important 2 = second important
Question 28	**When I think of myself as a personality, which two qualities are more typical for me than the others (BE HONEST)?**	
Y	Enterprising greed.	
F	Frequent phases of melancholy.	
T	Hidden flattery.	
N	Frequent self-forgetfulness.	
X	Clever deception.	
E	Hidden feelings of revenge.	
O	Quiet resentment.	
S	Evasive cautiousness/cowardice.	
Z	Joyful planning of the future.	

TOPIC	ENCOURAGEMENTS	1 = very important
Question 29	There are two specific encouragements that give me special power and strength that particularly build me up:	2 = second important
X	You're just as loved as you are!	
Y	Your needs are absolutely okay!	
E	You won't be cheated, nobody wants to hurt you!	
F	You're very special, you deserve recognition!	
S	You're totally safe, you can totally rely on it!	
N	You are important, deserve attention and love!	
T	You are wanted, desired and welcome!	
Z	You will be taken care of, no one will take away your joy of life!	
O	You are good and do not have to improve!	

TOPIC	ENERGETIC CHARISMA	1 = very important
Question 30	Which two aspects do I find especially in relation to my energetic charisma on other people?	2 = second important
X	I am a heart person and have a sober, objective charisma.	
N	I am a gut person and have an optimistic charisma.	
S	I am a head person and have an intense charisma.	
F	I am a heart person and have an intense charisma.	
O	I am a gut person and have a sober, objective charisma.	
Z	I am a head person and have an optimistic charisma.	
T	I am a heart person and have an optimistic charisma.	
E	I am a gut person and have an intense charisma.	
Y	I am a head person and have a sober, objective charisma.	

TOPIC	ENERGETIC QUALITY OF GAZING	1 = very important
Question 31	I look into the mirror in peace and look into my eyes! Which two gaze qualities do I particularly perceive right now?	2 = second important
F	Melancholic, sad, lost - deep, directed inwards.	
S	Anxious, careful, skeptical - bordering.	
Y	Thoughtful, intellectual, empty - distant.	
N	Gentle, peaceful, relaxed - peripheral.	
X	Focused, confident of victory, successful - outward-looking.	
Z	Lively, cheerful, optimistic - rather warm, bright.	
O	Precise, distant, critical - rather cool.	
E	Dominant, controlling, intimidating - rather cool.	
T	Lovingly caring, connecting - rather warm.	

TOPIC	ERRING LOVE	1 = very important
Question 32	My love sometimes goes astray and then expresses itself somewhat distorted especially in two of the following descriptions:	2 = second important
Z	Fun and joy instead of true love!	
T	Conditional love, help, care & give instead of true love!	
S	Reliability & loyalty instead of true love!	
X	Success and achievement instead of true love!	
Y	Knowledge, observation & distance instead of true love!	
F	Individuality and creativity instead of true love!	
E	Power, strength & control instead of true love!	
N	Harmony, peace & self-forgetfulness instead of true love!	
O	Perfection & correctness instead of true love!	

TOPIC	FACIAL EXPRESSIONS	1 = very important
Question 33	When I look in the mirror and perceive my facial expressions, how do I best describe them in two ways?	2 = second important
O	Frown, vertical wrinkle in the middle between the eyes, checking.	
X	Cool, unapproachable, emotionally a little "frozen", symmetrical.	
Y	Intellectual, "empty" facial expressions with horizontal forehead wrinkles.	
Z	Open, optimistic facial expressions, friendly, funny, mild, benevolent.	
N	Expressionless, self-forgetting, motionless, slow facial expressions.	
E	Controlling, present, powerful, strong, dominant facial expressions.	
S	Reserved, cautious, skeptical, doubting facial expressions.	
F	Emotionally intense, enigmatic and recondite facial expressions.	
T	Caring, attentive, maternal, concerned, benevolent facial expressions.	

TOPIC	FAITH/RELIGION/SPIRITUALITY	1 = very important
Question 34	I understand faith, religion and spirituality primarily under two of the following aspects:	2 = second important
E	Ordering, powerful authority, innocence, divine justice.	
F	Yearning for depth, arriving at home, creative source of power.	
Z	Promise of happiness, paradise, expression of the pure and the good.	
Y	An instance beyond knowledge, formless emptiness.	
T	Origin of divine, supportive humble love.	
O	Meaningful world view, expression of divine, paternal love.	
N	Common unity of ego-free love, the peace of God.	
S	Community-building character, faith and trust in God.	
X	Divine expression of creative-energetic, appreciative love.	

TOPIC	FEELINGS IN CHILDHOOD	1 = very important
Question 35	Which two basic feelings prevailed particularly in my childhood from my present point of view?	2 = second important
S	I often felt powerless, never allowed to make my own decisions.	
Y	Often I felt harassed, my privacy was not respected.	
O	I was criticized / punished and tried to be as good as possible.	
T	I was only loved when I helped others or gave them something.	
N	I remained unnoticed, my opinions and feelings were not important.	
Z	I had many fears and escaped into a world of dreams and imagination.	
F	I felt abandoned, got no emotional support.	
E	I had to stand up for myself and I wasn't allowed to show any weakness.	
X	I have always been especially praised for my achievements.	

TOPIC	FOCUS OF ATTENTION	1 = very important
Question 36	My special attention, my energy I focus on the following two main points:	2 = second important
Z	Positive, enjoyable alternatives!	
X	Achievement, who gives me recognition in the profession?	
Y	Requirements that are placed on me, what do they want from me?	
S	Intentions of others, which hidden intentions others have?	
N	Attitudes of others, what do the others think?	
F	The good in the missing, the bad in the existing!	
O	Right and wrong, what`s wrong with a situation?	
T	Personal recognition, who recognizes me as a human being?	
E	Control of others, who can I control?	

TOPIC	FOCUS POINTS IN MISBEHAVIOR	1 = very important
Question 37	Which two focal points in misbehavior are particularly typical for me when I am mentally unbalanced?	2 = second important
Y	I develop a one-sided hyperanalytic behavior and resign at times internally relatively fast.	
X	I play (fake) roles that don't quite suit me personally.	
E	I act excessively fast (and sometimes also imprudent).	
O	I tend to suppress my impulses through self-control.	
S	I tend to project things, seek out the culprit, etc.	
F	I develop a one-sided hypersensitive behavior and sometimes get into a state of bewilderment.	
T	I sometimes manipulate my fellow human beings, even if I only mean well for them.	
Z	I quickly plan one-sided intensively for the far future.	
N	I quickly enter a state of passivity and indifference.	

TOPIC	FURTHER DEVELOPMENT (TRANSFORMATION)	1 = very important
Question 38	Which two of the following topics are particularly central to my personal development?	2 = second important
O	Accept that life is perfect, perceive the positive, face one's own truths, allow hidden humor, expose oneself to life.	
F	To get to know the complexity of the soul, to seek the "YES" to life, to lift the inner, hidden treasures, to learn to love the profane, to understand the longing, to make the world a home.	
Y	Perceive emotions and live, play and dance, seek goals in life, explore the deep meaning, learn to love, build bridges to real life.	
S	Gain self-knowledge, seek out fear-triggering situations, avoid projections, not put up with everything, develop courage and confidence.	

Continued question 38 see next page …

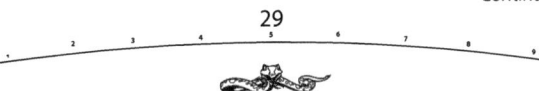

… continued question 38:

TOPIC	FURTHER DEVELOPMENT (TRANSFORMATION)	1 = very important
Question 38	**Which two of the following topics are particularly central to my personal development?**	2 = second important
Z	Paths to inner support, the inner center search, reality testing, more grip, staying with things.	
E	Creating a hierarchy of problems, feeling responsible for oneself, being strong through admitting weakness, recognizing egoism, giving strength to others and allowing others to do the same.	
N	Training conflict skills, experiencing oneself, recognizing the original, getting into the right action, overcoming auto-aggressiveness.	
X	Success must not be the primary value of life, no longer displace one's own truths, to conduct conversations with oneself, listening to one's inner voice.	
T	Not to relieve others of responsibility, to seek sense and silence, to find oneself, to pay attention to oneself, to help oneself, to recognize one's own needs.	

TOPIC	GARDENING	1 = very important
Question 39	**What does working in the garden mean most to me (two possibilities)?**	2 = second important
E	I do not leave the garden until everything is done!	
F	Everything well-balanced, suitable, atmospheric, creative garden design!	
T	I design the garden so that it is a meeting place!	
N	In itself quite beautiful and relaxing, but sometimes also exhausting!	
Y	First of all I get enough suggestions from my garden book!	
Z	When the weather is nice, I enjoy the work, otherwise I move it!	
X	The main thing, in the end it is beautiful and I get applause!	
O	Above all, the garden should be clean, well maintained and functional!	
S	I make sure that I can finish quickly, it could, for example, rain soon!	

TOPIC	GESTURES	1 = very important
Question 40	When I look at the totality of my gestures as an expression of my inner attitude, which two are particularly typical?	2 = second important
T	Connecting gestures, unconsciously seeks body contact with the hands.	
E	Present, energetic, exuberant, controlling gestures.	
O	"From above down", raised index finger, few but precise gestures.	
S	Wait-and-see, reserved, cautious, insecure, frozen gestures.	
X	Fast, jagged, erratic, sometimes sweeping gestures.	
N	Few gestures, overall low-movement posture.	
Z	Fleeting arm movements, slow, deliberate, open, communicative.	
F	Extravagant, elegant gestures, sweeping hand gestures.	
Y	Relatively little gesture, strong head movements (approving nodding).	

TOPIC	GIFT IDEAS	1 = very important
Question 41	Which two gift ideas could give me a special pleasure personally?	2 = second important
Y	a really interesting book	
X	definitely something valuable, magnificent	
O	a day planner	
S	a shared experience	
N	something I mentioned earlier	
Z	a living gift with an experience value	
E	best a money present	
F	something with a memory value	
T	a wellness day or weekend	

TOPIC	GO SHOPPING	1 = very important
Question 42	**Which two main considerations are most likely to go through my mind before or during shopping?**	2 = second important
N	I prefer to forget nothing, otherwise I have to go again!	
F	Let's see if I can find something nice, maybe something special!	
Z	Only when the shopping cart is full, then I am satisfied!	
T	I shop for all, so that the needs of all are satisfied!	
E	I shop less often, so when I go shopping I have to pack a lot to stock up!	
S	I make sure that I do not spend too much, let's see!	
Y	I buy as cheaply as possible, only the necessary, best offers!	
X	I like to shop fast, effectively, I do not pay attention to prices!	
O	Quality/a good price-performance ratio is important to me above all!	

TOPIC	IDENTIFICATION	1 = very important
Question 43	**Above all, I identify myself with two of the following descriptions of my personality:**	2 = second important
F	With the feeling of being different or "defective" and reacting emotionally.	
Z	With the feeling of anticipation of pleasant experiences.	
T	With the reactions of the people I could help.	
S	With the need for support and security.	
E	With the feeling of intensity that arises from defying others.	
N	With the feeling of inner stability due to the detachment from intense impulses.	
X	With a self-image that I create by playing a role that others admire.	
O	With the ability to evaluate and classify what has been experienced.	
Y	With the sensation of being an observer detached from the world.	

TOPIC	ILLNESS BEHAVIOR	1 = very important
Question 44	In case of illness, I move into the so-called stress point and develop in particular the following two behavioral tendencies:	2 = second important
Y	Fluttering, hyperactive, repressing, fleeing from suffering.	
T	Abusive, offensive, dominant, aggressive, domineering.	
F	Clinging, affectionate, intrusive, needy, dependent.	
O	Melancholic, jealous, moody, sad, rejecting, irrational.	
S	Acting actively, restless, driven, arrogant, ruthless.	
E	Withdrawn, distanced, analytical, anxious, closed.	
N	Overanxious, full of self-doubt, insecure, sceptical, doubting.	
Z	Nagging, perfectionist, know-it-all, insistent.	
X	Sluggish, aimless, disoriented, self-doubting, apathetic, closed-minded, withdrawn.	

TOPIC	INNER PRINCIPLES	1 = very important
Question 45	The following inner guiding principles may create inner resistances in me and thus prevent my personal development:	2 = second important
X	I should be successful!	
O	I should do the right thing!	
F	I should be a very special person!	
S	I should do my duty!	
Z	I should be happy!	
Y	I should keep my distance!	
E	I should be strong!	
N	I should live in harmony!	
T	I should help others!	

TOPIC	INTUITIVE STYLE	1 = very important
Question 46	Which two intuitive styles do I particularly prefer as a human and personality in my everyday life?	2 = second important
Y	I observe everything best from the objective metaposition.	
F	I perceive the moods of others directly and absorb them into myself.	
E	I can sense the degree of power.	
O	I wonder how perfect the situation could be?	
S	In order to fathom all the circumstances, I like to fantasize mentally.	
T	I adapt to the needs of my fellow human beings.	
N	I merge, mingle with the others, search for unity.	
X	I sometimes disguise myself in order to achieve my goals.	
Z	I easily form mental connections, can associate well.	

TOPIC	JESUS CHRIST ASPECTS	1 = very important
Question 47	I can identify myself particularly well with two of the following nine aspects relating to Jesus:	2 = second important
S	The loyal citizen who wisely dodges political catch questions.	
X	The victor who resists the temptations of the devil.	
Z	Jesus was not an ascetic, but he liked to celebrate and did not fast.	
N	The peacemaker who calls to the weary and loaded and encourages them, or the sleeping one in the midst of the storm.	
Y	The son who sets himself apart from his parents and calls his disciples "mother and brothers".	
F	His eye for the beauties of nature such as the famous "lilies in the field", which are dressed more splendidly than King Solomon.	
E	The determined preacher who provocatively expelled the merchants from the temple.	
O	His uncompromising interpretation of the 10 Commandments in the Sermon on the Mount.	
T	His healings of the sick and needy, even on the Sabbath.	

TOPIC	LANGUAGE STYLES	1 = very important
Question 48	Which two language styles do I prefer in my everyday language use?	2 = second important
O	Instructive, moralizing, ready for press, admonishing, corrective, chosen, technical language, correct expressions.	
S	Warning, limiting, questioning, cautious, testing, doubting, quiet.	
Z	Chatty, babbling, easy, evasive, animating, narrative.	
F	Lyrical, lamenting, aesthetic, pictorial, enigmatic, spherical, nebulous, emotional, illogical, emotionally fluctuating.	
X	Advertising, inspiring, motivating, appealing, striking linguistic melody, accentuated, creating attention through language.	
E	Challenging, unmasking, direct, clear, deep, powerful voice, loud (quiet = it gets dangerous!).	
T	Flattering, advising, kind, benevolent, cordial, trivializing.	
N	Monotonous, digressive, quiet, no modulation in the voice.	
Y	Explanatory, systematizing, curious, interested, sober, calm language, well-considered, taking breaks, talkative or silent.	

TOPIC	LIFE OR LEARNING TASKS	1 = very important
Question 49	In my opinion, which two things do I particularly have to understand or transform in my life?	2 = second important
N	Self oblivion & numbness in self-confidence & responsibility.	
E	Hardness & rigorousness in goodness & generosity.	
Z	Avoidance of suffering and pain in a sober cheerfulness.	
T	Pride & exaggerated willingness to help in true love & humility.	
S	Fear & distrust/doubt in courage & trust/faith.	
Y	Knowledge, analysis & distance in wisdom & emotional closeness.	
X	Lies & deception in truthfulness & clarity.	
F	Homelessness & lostness in authenticity.	
O	Impatience & irritability in patience and serenity.	

TOPIC	LONGINGS	1 = very important
Question 50	If I am honest, which two fundamental longings are the most important to me?	2 = second important
X	To be myself (to be allowed to be myself) and after truthfulness.	
S	For courage and freedom from anxiety.	
N	To be seen and to act properly.	
T	For love, being loved and humility.	
Y	For omniscience and non-attachment.	
E	For mental balance and for truth.	
F	For home, to find yourself and for equanimity.	
Z	For abundance and sober enjoyment of life.	
O	For perfection and (cheerful) serenity.	

TOPIC	LOVE (EXPRESSIONS)	1 = very important
Question 51	My love is expressed, above all, in two of the following expressions:	2 = second important
S	Friendly-faithful or combative-antagonistic love (unstable)	
F	Romantic-consuming love (unfulfilled)	
T	Maternal-supporting love (interpersonal)	
O	Paternal-promoting love (perfect)	
E	Combative-fighting love (body-oriented)	
Z	Playful-humorous love (naive, easy)	
N	Sibling-accepting love (harmonious-equivalent)	
Y	Spiritual-platonic love (idealizing, lonely)	
X	Creative-energetic love (formal, outward)	

TOPIC	LOVE RELATIONSHIPS & LOVE STYLES	1 = very important
Question 52	In the love relationship with a partner, I act mainly in the following two ways:	2 = second important
Z	I'm looking for joy in the relationship, want to distract you so you'll be happy again. If you are depressed, then I am not so happy to be with you - lustful love!	
S	I feel safer being the giver because I don't really know your motives for giving me anything. I'm slowly learning to trust you - submissive or patronizing love!	
Y	I prefer to hold back my deep feelings when we are together, because I have to protect myself somehow. When I'm alone, I think of you a lot - indifferent love!	
F	I'm looking forward to you, but when you get there, it's hard for me to live in the present moment. I want something, but I don't know what. I`m scared to love you deeply because I could get hurt - morbid love!	

TOPIC	MAIN CHARACTERISTICS	1 = very important
Question 53	Two of the following main characteristics of my character - if I am honest - are particularly pronounced in me:	2 = second important
F	melancholy, envy, feeling of deficiency	
Z	planning, insatiability, immoderateness	
N	inertia, comfort, slowness	
O	resentment, anger, upset	
S	paranoia, doubt, mistrust	
X	efficiency, deception, lies	
E	retribution, lust, intensity	
T	flattery, pride, influence	
Y	reclusiveness, avarice, greed	

TOPIC	MAIN DEMANDS	1 = very important
Question 54	What is particularly important to me in the interpersonal exchange with my fellow human being?	2 = second important
Z	Satisfied, positive, contented, not disadvantaged.	
F	To understand oneself, to be understood, to be stylish, to be creative.	
S	To receive security, guarantees, feeling of security, to recognize the intentions of others.	
N	To feel satisfied, connected with others, harmonious and comfortable.	
O	To be right, to observe morality, ethics, accuracy, criticism.	
X	To be accepted, valued, admired and desired.	
Y	To understand the environment and life, to be competent and wise.	
E	To be strong, fair, competent, self-reliant and independent.	
T	To be loved, to be attentive, to flatter, to help.	

TOPIC	MANIPULATION STRATEGIES	1 = very important
Question 55	Which two manipulation strategies do I prefer in everyday life (BE HONEST):	2 = second important
T	I research the needs of others to create dependencies.	
E	I dominate others, intimidate them, threaten and demand the observance of my instructions.	
Y	I show myself lost in thought and give others the feeling of being incompetent in order to keep them emotionally at a distance.	
X	I adapt to the other person in the best possible way and choose every image that "works".	
N	I withdraw, go out of contact, I`m unapproachable, aloof, resist passively aggressive.	
S	I complain, criticize and test the loyalty I have received.	
F	I tend to behave like a mimosa, forcing consideration.	

Continued question 55 see next page …

TOPIC	MANIPULATION STRATEGIES	1 = very important
Question 55	**Which two manipulation strategies do I prefer in everyday life (BE HONEST):**	2 = second important
O	I correct others, point out their badness and mistakes and insist on the generality of my opinion.	
Z	I distract myself or others to avoid unpleasant feelings or situations and insist on the fulfillment of my wishes.	

TOPIC	MASKS	1 = very important
Question 56	**Which two masks do I wear most frequently towards my fellow human beings?**	2 = second important
Z	Always optimistic, enthusiastic, happy, easy-going, lively, vibrant, positive, spontaneous, sociable, vigorous, positive, energetic.	
N	Always peace-loving, peaceful, serene, stable, gentle, relaxed, friendly, balanced, natural, calm.	
O	Always blameless, impeccable, rational, temperate, moderate, "good", insightful, intelligent, rational, objective, moral, ethical, standing above things.	
X	Always competent, admirable, outstanding, desirable, attractive, successful, self-confident, tireless, sure of victory.	
Y	Always objective, insightful, restrained, sensitive, attentive, witty, curious, intelligent.	
E	Always strong, robust, imaginative, independent, direct, persistent, action-oriented, ready for action.	
S	Always courageous, reliable, foresighted, "in order", trustworthy, careful, endearing.	
T	Always generous, loving, well-considered, empathic, warm-hearted, compassionate, selfless, concerned, passionate, kind.	
F	Always authentic, profound, sensitive, self-critical, in depth, different, sincere, unique, intuitive, meek, gentle.	

TOPIC	MONEY PROFIT	1 = very important
Question 57	**With a tax-free cash lottery prize of $ 2 million, I would do two things above all else:**	2 = second important
F	Promote my artistic existence through financial independence.	
S	Support my own family or my association.	
E	Building something big, realizing a big project.	
X	Have the freedom to successfully actualize my success.	
O	Make the world a better place through projects.	
Y	Set up a research lab or open a bookstore.	
Z	Travel, adventure, celebrate, live well, have a good time.	
T	Bring aid projects into being, support aid organizations.	
N	Relax, without pressure, without obligations, just be there.	

TOPIC	MOTIVATIONS FOR MY ACTIONS	1 = very important
Question 58	**Which two deeper motives are the true causes of my actions (I listen deep inside myself)?**	2 = second important
F	The eternal search for individuality and uniqueness.	
S	The eternal search for security and trust.	
T	The eternal search for love and being loved.	
E	The eternal search for power and control.	
N	The eternal search for harmony and peace.	
Z	The eternal search for fun and enjoyment of life.	
Y	The eternal search for knowledge and wisdom.	
O	The eternal search for perfection and completeness.	
X	The eternal search for success and achievement.	

TOPIC	MOTIVATIONS, AVOIDANCE & PASSIONS	1 = very important
Question 59	The interaction of motivation, avoidance and passion is particularly characteristic for me in the two following cases:	2 = second important
Y	Motivation knowledge - avoidance of emptiness - passion: avarice.	
E	Motivation power - avoidance of weakness - passion: greed.	
N	Motivation harmony - avoidance of conflict - passion: inertia.	
X	Motivation success - avoidance of failure - passion: vanity.	
F	Motivation: individuality - avoidance of being ordinary - passion: envy.	
T	Motivation: love - avoidance of neediness - passion: pride.	
O	Motivation: perfection - avoidance of mistakes - passion: anger.	
Z	Motivation: fun - avoidance of pain - passion: gluttony.	
S	Motivation: safety - avoidance of deviant behavior - passion: fear.	

TOPIC	MOTTOS OF LIFE	1 = very important
Question 60	Which two mottos of life particularly appeal to me inwardly, which generate a deep resonance in me?	2 = second important
S	Courage instead of fear!	
Y	Openness instead of avarice!	
F	Authenticity instead of envy!	
X	Truthfulness instead of vanity!	
T	Love instead of pride!	
O	Patience instead of anger!	
Z	Sobriety instead of gluttony!	
E	Goodness instead of lust!	
N	Responsibility instead of inertia!	

TOPIC	MUSICAL TASTE	1 = very important
Question 61	For me, good music is especially characterized by two of the following points:	2 = second important
X	Solemn, rhythmic, popular sounds.	
Y	Entertaining, calm sounds.	
Z	Cheerful, lighthearted, lively, playful sounds.	
N	Relaxing, calm, balancing, harmonious sounds.	
T	Connecting, emotional, lovely, healing sounds.	
F	Emotional depth, real, authentic, romantic sounds.	
S	Folksy, proven sounds carried by a sense of security.	
E	Powerful, uplifting, emotive, dominant sounds.	
O	Harmonious composition, straightforwardness, structured sounds.	

TOPIC	NATURAL PHENOMENA	1 = very important
Question 62	I particularly like two of the following natural phenomena:	2 = second important
N	All seasons, each in its own way in natural change.	
E	The forces of nature, extreme weather conditions, the power of nature.	
Z	The sun shining through the treetops, tasty fruits and the colorful variety of blossoms.	
T	Medicinal plants & herbs, biodiversity of animals and plants.	
X	The splendor of colors, the beauty and the variety of forms of nature.	
F	Atmospheric sunsets by the sea and the wide view of the horizon.	
O	Well-kept parks, English lawns, the natural order of nature.	
S	The whole ecosystem, how everything interacts with each other.	
Y	The laws of nature and the complex interaction of all factors.	

TOPIC	NEEDS (SUBJECTIVELY FELT)	1 = very important
Question 63	Which two needs in my life are of central importance to me?	2 = second important
S	to be safe and protected	
T	to be loved, to be indispensable	
O	to be right, to have integrity, to be good and virtuous	
Y	to be able to understand the world, a need to be competent	
F	to be able to understand yourself, to be someone with meaning	
N	for unity and harmony, to have peace of mind	
X	to be recognized by others, useful, popular, desired	
Z	for satisfaction, for happiness and fulfillment	
E	for independence, to protect yourself	

TOPIC	NEW YEAR WISHES	1 = very important
Question 64	Which two of the following New Year wishes would suit me best?	2 = second important
E	Don't ALWAYS just set the tone and don't ALWAYS strive for power & control!	
Z	Don't ALWAYS look for the positive and don't ALWAYS strive for fun & joy!	
S	Don't ALWAYS be cautious and suspicious, don't constantly doubt and don't ALWAYS strive for safety!	
Y	Don`t ALWAYS try to understand the world and don`t ALWAYS strive for knowledge!	
F	Don't ALWAYS try to understand yourself and don't ALWAYS strive for individuality!	
X	Don't ALWAYS search for recognition and don't ALWAYS strive for success!	

Continued question 64 see next page …

TOPIC Question 64		1 = very important 2 = second important
T	Don`t ALWAYS pay attention only to the needs of others and don`t ALWAYS strive for love and being loved!	
O	Don´t ALWAYS be impeccable, don`t be right CONSTANTLY and don`t ALWAYS strive for perfection!	
N	Don`t ALWAYS adapt, don`t ONLY be calm, balanced and peaceful and don`t ALWAYS strive for harmony!	

TOPIC Question 65	ONE-SIDED ATTITUDES Which of the following two human one-sided attitudes have often led me to dead ends (BE HONEST)?	1 = very important 2 = second important
S	anxiety, fear, doubt, mistrust	
O	rage, anger, upset, resentment	
X	deception, lies, deceit, vanity	
Y	greed, cupidity, avarice, distance	
N	inertia, comfort, laziness, passivity	
Z	insatiability, intemperance, gluttony	
F	melancholy, sadness, inner lack, envy	
T	imagination, complacency, arrogance, pride	
E	lust, shamelessness, excess, compulsion to control	

TOPIC	PARTY BEHAVIOR (BEFORE, DURING AND AFTER THE PARTY)	1 = very important
Question 66	Which thoughts do I usually have <u>before</u>, <u>during</u> and <u>after</u> a party, which two attitudes are especially typical for me?	2 = second important
T	**Before:** I hope everyone likes me! **During:** I like to help in the kitchen or at the buffet! **After:** I totally exhausted myself, but I'm glad that everyone got along so well!	
Y	**Before:** I would rather stay at home, sit on the couch and read my book! **During:** Somehow I don't seem to be able to get into intellectual conversation! **After:** Fortunately, I managed to leave early and find time to continue reading my book!	
E	**Before:** If wine, woman and song are not right, I am gone! **During:** This idiot should not get upset because I`ve just given him what is my own opinion! **After:** I had to make it unequivocally clear again who the boss is!	
Z	**Before:** If the mood is flat, I`ll still have other irons in the fire! **During:** It`s a little boring here, let's see what other parties there are! **After:** I had great fun at the 3rd party, but the night is still young!	
F	**Before:** I'm not in the mood for a party at all! **During:** The buffet is quite ordinary, what is there to eat here? **After:** Most of the conversations were quite trivial!	
O	**Before:** Hopefully I will bring the right wine! **During:** The food is not balanced enough! **After:** Hopefully I have not offended anyone with my comments!	
N	**Before:** It would be great if I met someone nice tonight! **During:** I feel so close to everyone, everyone is nice and friendly to me! **After:** I think everyone loved my stories and remember me well!	
S	**Before:** I must not forget to feed the cat and lock up! **During:** Did I just talk too much, why did she make this remark? **After:** It's great to be back home safely.	
X	**Before:** Tonight I want to bring the right people together! **During:** Just eat fast, then I'll be gone! I am totally overloaded! **After:** I was able to make very good contacts while eating!	

TOPIC	PASSIONS	1 = very important
Question 67	Which two passions (characteristics) are particularly unpleasant to me?	2 = second important
O	Anger/annoyance/resentment - "addicted" to perfection.	
T	Pride/haughtiness/loftiness - "addicted" to personal recognition.	
X	Vanity/glory - "addicted" to rocognition for achievement/success.	
F	Envy/sadness/selfishness - "addicted" to self-knowledge.	
Y	Avarice/stinginess - "addicted" to knowledge/world understanding.	
S	Anxiety/Fear/Cowardice - "addicted" to safety/certainty.	
Z	Gluttony/excessiveness/search for happiness - "addicted" to the joy of life.	
E	Lust/greed/striving for power - "addicted" to strength/dominance/control.	
N	Inertia (of the heart)/convenience ("addicted" to harmony/satisfaction).	

TOPIC	POLARITIES	1 = very important
Question 68	Which polarities of life do you feel familiar with, in which context do you find yourself?	2 = second important
S	Submitting - determining; honest - supercritical.	
E	Hedonic - puritanical; self-confident - power obsessed.	
O	Rigid - sensitive; reliable - dogmatic.	
F	Analytical - disoriented; sensitive - moody.	
Y	Unsociable - sociable; objective - snobbish.	
Z	Superior - inferior; lightness of being - narcissistic.	
N	Believing - doubtful; calm - phlegmatic.	
X	Overactive - imaginative; dynamic - status obsessed.	
T	Rampant - militant; empathetic - unstable.	

TOPIC	POSITIVE AFFIRMATIONS	1 = very important
Question 69	When I consciously read through the following positive affirmations, which two touch me emotionally in particular?	2 = second important
X	You're loved just the way you are!	
F	You deserve recognition!	
Y	Your needs are okay!	
T	You're welcome!	
O	You're good!	
N	You're important!	
E	You won't be cheated!	
Z	You'll be taken care of!	
S	You're safe!	

TOPIC	PROBLEM SITUATIONS	1 = very important
Question 70	How do I prefer to behave in problem situations (please choose two alternatives again)?	2 = second important
N	I withdraw and offer passive-aggressive resistance.	
O	I correct others and insist on the correctness of my ideas.	
E	I dominate others and demand compliance with my instructions.	
T	I explore the needs of my fellow human beings in order to create dependencies through my role as a helper.	
Z	I distract others and insist on fulfilling my wishes.	
X	I adapt and choose every image that works.	
S	I complain and test the loyalty I have received.	
F	I behave like a mimosa, in order to enforce consideration.	
Y	I'm often lost in thought, keep emotional distance.	

TOPIC	PROFESSIONAL PRACTICE	1 = very important
Question 71	In my profession the following two aspects are of special importance to me:	2 = second important
O	improving the world	
Y	expertise and skills	
N	relaxed activity or routine work	
T	helping others	
F	spiritual vocation	
Z	self-realization or varied activity	
E	exercise of authority / control over others	
X	social status	
S	secure employment	

TOPIC	PROGRAMMINGS OF THE PERSONALITY	1 = very important
Question 72	Which two unconscious "programmings" do you find particularly pronounced in you personally (BE HONEST)?	2 = second important
E	self-righteousness & hidden arrogance	
T	helpfulness & hidden manipulation	
F	exceptionality & sentimentality	
O	perfection & inner resentment	
Z	carefree optimism & nervous activity	
Y	knowledge advantage & retreat	
S	safety orientation & anxious doubts	
X	striving for achievement & image care	
N	peacefulness & inert indecisiveness	

TOPIC	PSYCHODYNAMIC CYCLE	1 = very important
Question 73	Which two inner-psychic dynamics are strangely familiar to you, which two particularly correspond to your personality?	2 = second important
O	The need to be right leads to the search for truth and correctness - CORRECTION - fear of being condemned, others are corrected, the need to be right ...	
T	The need to be loved leads to helping others - LOVE - fear of not being loved, unforgiving and manipulating others, the need to be loved ...	
X	The need to be admired leads to self-improvement - ADMIRATION - fear of rejection, pressure to succeed and competition, the need to be admired ...	
F	The need to understand oneself leads to self-enquiry - SELF UNDERSTANDING - fear of being inadequate, indulge in fantasies, the need to understand oneself ...	
Y	The need to understand the world leads to observation, analysis - WORLD UNDERSTANDING - fear of being overwhelmed by the world, detached, disconnected from the world and others, the need to understand the world ...	
S	The need for security leads to the loyalty to others - SECURITY - fear of being abandoned, distrust of others, the need for security ...	
Z	The need to be happy leads to exploring, enjoying and treasuring the material world - ENJOYMENT OF LIFE - fear of being deprived of happiness, seeking positive sensations and avoiding suffering, the need to be happy ...	
E	The need to be independent leads to great strength and power - INDEPENDENCE - fear of being subject to others, controlling others and oneself, the need to be independent ...	
N	The need to connect leads to acceptance - UNITY - fear of separation, adapting to others - the need to connect ...	

TOPIC	ROLE PATTERNS - HEAD, HEART OR GUT INSTINCT	1 = very important
Question 74	**In which characteristic two role patterns do I personally recognize myself the most?**	2 = second important
F	creative individualist, romanticist, aesthete - heart instinct	
Y	researching thinker, specialist, discerning observer - head instinct	
X	friendly success person, impulse generator, catalyst - heart instinct	
S	loyal protector, persevering, questioner - head instinct	
T	good-natured advisor, altruist, helper - heart instinct	
Z	entertaining optimist, generalist, enthusiast - head instinct	
O	patient moralist, perfectionist, organizer - gut instinct	
E	protective challenger, pragmatist, realist - gut instinct	
N	peaceable mediator, harmony-oriented, tolerant - gut instinct	

TOPIC	SELF-IMAGE	1 = very important
Question 75	**If I go deep into myself and feel into myself there, which two self-images do I find confirmed there above all?**	2 = second important
E	I am powerful, strong and invincible!	
O	I'm doing it right and I'm right!	
X	I am successful and focused!	
Y	I recognize my environment through observation and reflection!	
Z	I am happy, active, cheerful, positive and optimistic!	
N	I am satisfied, relaxed and affable!	
T	I am helpful and loving!	
S	I am faithful and do my duty!	
F	I am different from others, sensitive and unique!	

TOPIC	SENSE OF SELF	1 = very important
Question 76	If I go deep into my heart with my consciousness, which two variants of a sense of self do I discover there?	2 = second important
N	I am peace-loving!	
S	I am adorable!	
X	I am desirable!	
T	I am loving!	
Y	I am knowledgeable!	
E	I am strong!	
F	I am sensitive!	
Z	I am happy!	
O	I am reasonable!	

TOPIC	SPECIAL ANXIETIES (FEARS)	1 = very important
Question 77	Which two things am I particularly afraid of, which two topics do I fear the most?	2 = second important
F	To be abandoned, to be lost and to be defective.	
N	To provoke a conflict and to be separated from others.	
E	To be weak and dependent and inferior to others.	
S	To be let down and afraid to be scared.	
Y	To be overwhelmed by the world and to lose something.	
Z	To be overworked, to suffer pain, to be deprived of happiness.	
O	To be condemned, for not being enough and for making mistakes.	
X	To be worthless, to have failure and not to receive recognition.	
T	To not be loved and to be rejected.	

TOPIC	SPECIAL AVERSIONS	1 = very important
Question 78	There are two following areas in my life, though I personally have a very special aversion:	2 = second important
T	Not being recognized, rejection, unfriendly, inattentive behavior.	
E	Lack of respect, injustice, subservience.	
N	Disagreement, discussion, changes, tensions.	
O	Economical execution, laxity, irresponsibility.	
X	Inefficiency, failure, loss of face.	
F	What others seem to have, lack of sensitivity, everyday life.	
Z	Limitations, routine, anything that is not fun, hurts, suffering means.	
S	Unreliability, ambiguity, not knowing where you stand.	
Y	Confused thinking, chaos, emotional reactions, lack of structure, too many expectations.	

TOPIC	SPECIAL PREFERENCES	1 = very important
Question 79	There are two following areas in my life, for which I personally have a very special preference:	2 = second important
T	Helpfulness, presence, friendliness.	
F	Authenticity, depth, sensitivity.	
X	Speed, success, self-confidence.	
O	Quality, responsible people, honesty.	
Y	Intelligence, respect for each other's space, careful use of language.	
S	Loyalty, clarity, openness.	
Z	Optimism, variety, possibilities.	
E	Directness, empowerment, justice.	
N	Harmony, stability, calm.	

TOPIC	SPORTS INTEREST	1 = very important
Question 80	Which two particular aspects of sport personally fascinate me?	2 = second important
S	Sports broadcasts on TV.	
Z	Sportive fun with the athletes and fans.	
E	Power and full commitment.	
Y	Scientific basis for body control.	
F	Expression of the body.	
X	Competition among the best.	
T	Comradeship and friendship despite the competition.	
O	Perfection and discipline.	
N	The all connecting athletic spirit.	

TOPIC	STATEMENTS (NON-VERBAL)	1 = very important
Question 81	In which two of the following non-verbal statements do I recognize myself best?	2 = second important
Z	Bright, enthusiastic eye expression, laughs or smiles again and again, lively and cheerful, mostly positive charisma.	
F	Appears energetically more inwardly focused and intense, moist, watery eye expression, sometimes looking lost, intense, sometimes very elegant appearance.	
S	Fast moving eyes, as if they are "palpating" the other, increases alert, tense posture, intense charisma.	
T	Often rounded shoulders with slightly sunken chest, warm eye expression, eyes looking for interpersonal contact, smiling to connect with each other.	
O	Tense jaw which holds back anger, self-controlled, upright posture ("stick swallowed!").	

Continued question 81 see next page …

… continued question 81:

TOPIC Question 81	STATEMENTS (NON-VERBAL) In which two of the following non-verbal statements do I recognize myself best?	1 = very important 2 = second important
N	Minimal facial expression, serene eye expression, motionless, relaxed, casual, but facing posture.	
E	Authoritarian-dominant and strong-acting with intense physical presence, grounded, almost immobile, direct eye contact with a firm, controlling look.	
X	Shoulders more horizontally aligned than rounded, energetic attention is concentrated in the face as well as in the upper body, confident, focused appearance.	
Y	Eye expression knowingly and thoughtfully focused inwards, as if one were observing oneself, head seems energetically independent of the body ("like a buoy swimming on the sea"), little grounded, frequent nodding of the head.	

TOPIC Question 82	STATEMENTS (VERBAL) In which of the following verbal statements do I recognize myself best?	1 = very important 2 = second important
Z	Fast, spontaneous language, euphoric, optimistic choice of words, telling exciting stories.	
F	Often shares personal things with others, frequently using the words "I", "me", "my", "mine," "as far as I'm concerned" etc., well considered.	
S	Hesitant or thoughtful speech, frequent use of doubtful questions, e.g. "What if? What happened if", abstract use of language.	
T	Frequent questions to others, soft, gentle voice, except when annoyed, compliments and flatters others.	
O	Repeatedly uses judgmental, unconditional words, e.g. "should", "must", "right", "wrong", "must", "would I do best" etc., frequently expresses opinions, uses a very precise language.	

Continued question 82 see next page …

… continued question 82:

TOPIC	STATEMENTS (VERBAL)	1 = very important
Question 82	In which of the following verbal statements do I recognize myself best?	2 = second important
Y	Lengthy, insightful explanations (if he knows the subject), but mostly quiet rather than talkative, minimal use of language.	
E	Rough, vulgar language, body-oriented humor, short, simple sentences, gives orders and controls the environment verbally.	
X	Wants to get to the topic/point verbally quickly, logical, clear and precise language, often presents ideas effectively in three (or a few) steps.	
N	Gives very detailed information, uses agreeing, appeasing words like "okay", "understand", "oh so" etc., answers completely, slowly, extensively and uniformly.	

TOPIC	STATEMENTS OF OTHERS ABOUT ME	1 = very important
Question 83	Two statements that others might make about me (and that might be strangely familiar to me):	2 = second important
F	Do not prevent your true happiness by your constant longing for something that does not exist!	
O	Your high standards cannot do you and others justice!	
Z	Do not always fade out everything negative in your life!	
X	You are loved for your own sake!	
T	You are not as selfless as you think, so do not expect others to give you anything in return for your love and care!	
E	You do not always have to set the tone!	
N	Take yourself and your needs seriously!	
Y	Do not be afraid of closeness and intense relationships, your needs are o.k.!	
S	In fearful phases of your life, have confidence in yourself and the world and give up the permanent struggle in courageous phases!	

TOPIC	STATEMENTS OF THE PARTNER (NEGATIVE)	1 = very important
Question 84	**Which two (negative) statements of the partner or possibly other close fellow human beings do I tend to hear more often?**	2 = second important
T	You do not always have to make me love you, show me what you need in matters of the heart!	
N	I wish sometimes you'd say what *you* want!	
F	When we get really close, you often push me away!	
E	You quickly find fault with me, you find it hard to apologize and your fits of rage are often unbearable!	
O	You criticize me very often, please accept that I am not perfect!	
Z	If I want to talk about my problems, you turn away!	
Y	When I get too close to you, you're always completely withdrawing!	
S	You are sometimes sarcastic and domineering and withdraw quickly when you become too insecure about me!	
X	You never show me your true face, your work is always more important, show me what you really feel!	

TOPIC	STATEMENTS OF THE PARTNER (POSITIVE)	1 = very important
Question 85	**Which two (positive) statements of the partner or possibly other close fellow human beings do I tend to hear more often?**	2 = second important
T	You make me feel special, you are generous and loving.	
N	You support me, you're friendly, soft-hearted, you don't judge. You understand my point of view.	
F	I like your sense of beauty, your humor, your passion and kindness. You understand me, listen to me.	
E	You are open, honest, faithful, caring and dedicated.	
O	You are humorous, honest, loyal, demanding and often communicate with heart and soul.	
Z	You are loving, generous, carefree, it is great fun with you.	
Y	You're knowledgeable, trustworthy, objective, I can talk to you well.	
S	You always hold to me, you're warm, fair and very humorous.	
X	You're responsible, generous, and I like your playfulness.	

TOPIC	STRENGTHS/QUALITIES	1 = very important
Question 86	Which two of the following strengths/qualities do I possess in a special way?	2 = second important
Z	idealism & optimism	
O	perfection & sense of responsibility	
F	authenticity & individualism	
S	security & loyalty	
E	justice & good protector	
N	acceptance & adaptability	
T	helpfulness & generosity	
X	efficiency and dynamics	
Y	power of observation & inquisitiveness	

TOPIC	STRESS REACTIONS	1 = very important
Question 87	In times of stress, I automatically react to two of the following typical behavioral patterns:	2 = second important
Y	Very retiring, exhausted, brooding, even more in the head, emotionally even more isolated, angry, depressed.	
O	Quickly irritated, effervescent, fuse can blow through, tense muscles, short of breath, offensive, angry, growling.	
S	Worrying even more, very anxious, even during minor situation, exhausted, full of self-doubt, angry to aggressive.	
T	Sleepless, anxious, insecure, unloved, discouraged, disappointed, sometimes hidden or openly angry.	
E	Excessive in all areas of life, restless sleep, workaholism, very aggressive, controlling, constant buying, withdrawing.	
X	Zealous, driven, dismissive, curt, sometimes hostile, verbally aggressive, anxious, isolated, lethargic.	

Continued question 87 see next page …

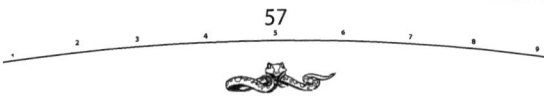

... continued question 87:

TOPIC	STRESS REACTIONS	1 = very important
Question 87	In times of stress, I automatically react to two of the following typical behavioral patterns:	2 = second important
N	Quiet or very talkative, greater need for sleep, becomes slow, forgetful, irritable, stubborn, refuses things, fruitless action.	
F	Moody, calm, self-centered, accusing, depressed, extremely irritated, stunned, lamenting to angry.	
Z	Manic to depressed, very talkative, communicative or totally calm, very anxious, angry, accusing.	

TOPIC	STYLES OF SPEECH	1 = very important
Question 88	Which two styles of speech do I prefer in my everyday language?	2 = second important
O	Preaching, speaking to provoke the conscience, drawing attention to misconduct.	
Z	Telling stories, lively, exciting, fascinating, entertaining, mild.	
N	Novel, telling "around the bush", little defined.	
S	Drawing boundaries, often in the subjunctive, friendly-tolerant.	
E	Paternalism, excluding free decisions, determining.	
Y	Essay, objective, matter-of-fact, sober, scientific, emotionally poor.	
X	Propaganda, spreading ideas, advertising, shaping, conning.	
T	Advising, verbal-supporting, recommending, manipulative.	
F	Lamentation, emotionally pessimistic, emphasis on lack and loss.	

TOPIC	SUBTYPE DESCRIPTIONS	1 = very important
Question 89	In which two of the following subtype descriptions do I at least find a suitable description for me?	2 = second important
Z	a) I enjoy the fun, the food and drink and the family. b) I limit myself and make sacrifices for the community. c) Ideas, people and products fascinate and influence me.	
Y	a) My home is my place of retreat, my "room with a view!" b) I live in my own mental world and looking for social symbols & systems. c) I treat people and things with great confidentiality.	
E	a) I protect and control the space and the family. b) I am strongly committed to friends and the social group. c) I have a strong tendency to possess (including people).	
T	a) I feel privileged and gain recognition for my services to people. b) I seek human recognition through great ambition. c) I use seduction or aggression to get attention.	
F	a) I am ruthless in the pursuit of authenticity. b) I overcome my social shame every day. c) I compete through strength or style.	
O	a) I overcome my anxiety through hard work and self-perfection. b) I am socially correct, but I am not adaptable. c) I am often over-greedy, immoderate or very jealous.	
X	a) I achieve and strive for success and financial security. b) I strive for social success and prestige. c) I have the best female or male image.	
N	a) I have a great appetite for food and possessions. b) Despite my high level of resilience, I have problems with equal participation in social groups. c) I strive for sexual and spiritual union, I have an inner urge to merge with other people.	
S	a) I seek security through warmth and benevolent affection. b) I fulfill my duties conscientiously and faithfully. c) I overcome fear by maintaining strength & beauty.	

TOPIC	SYMBOLIC ARCHETYPE	1 = very important
Question 90	With which two symbolic figures (archetypes) can I best identify spontaneously?	2 = second important
X	the wonderful magician	
Y	the mystical philosopher	
E	the mighty warrior	
O	the righteous ruler	
T	the divine mother	
F	the great artist	
S	the courageous hero	
Z	the magic child	
N	the gentle saint	

TOPIC	THREATS (SUBJECTIVELY FELT)	1 = very important
Question 91	Which two threats of life represent a special challenge for me?	2 = second important
O	Perfection threatened.	
N	Being threatened.	
Y	Security threatened.	
T	Needs threatened.	
E	Control threatened.	
X	Self-esteem threatened.	
Z	Enjoyment (of life) threatened.	
S	Self-confidence, faith threatened.	
F	Self threatened.	

TOPIC	TRAPS	1 = very important
Question 92	Each enneatype can take a characteristic wrong path in its search for meaning, which two are above all with me?	2 = second important
X	Competing with others, vanity, outwardness, more appearance than being!	
T	Good intentions, flattery, courtesy, manipulate fellow human beings!	
E	Set the tone, take the lead, take the room!	
S	Become dependent on others, show cowardice or recklessness!	
N	Harmony at any price, just no conflicts, convenience!	
O	To fulfill my duty, to be sensitive, inwardly irritated, rigid!	
F	Escape into fantasies, melancholy, strongly compare me with others!	
Z	Want to have everything, plan too much, hide negative things!	
Y	Want to analyze everything, stinginess, emotional withdrawal/distance!	

TOPIC	TRAVEL	1 = very important
Question 93	Especially two of the following motives are decisive for me again and again for a journey:	2 = second important
Z	Adventure, discoveries, change, variety of impressions, fun.	
S	Thoroughly explore your own home, vacation packages.	
F	Finding inspiration in foreign cultures, experiencing something unique.	
X	Famous places and luxurious accommodation are important to me.	
N	To let yourself be pampered, to have a good night's rest, to relax.	
Y	To observe and get to know a lot of new things, discover interesting things.	
O	To understand the cultural and ideological differences.	
T	To get to know and love foreign people in peripheral areas as well.	
E	To undertake daring adventures, go your own way, feel your own strength.	

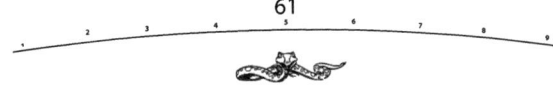

TOPIC Question 94	**TRUE VALUES** **Which true values, in my opinion, should I - if I am completely honest - personally develop?**	1 = very important 2 = second important
N	Responsibility and right action instead of inertia of the heart.	
T	Love and humility instead of subliminal pride.	
Z	Sobriety and a sense of reality instead of gluttony and distraction.	
F	Authenticity and mental balance instead of envy and hypersensitivity.	
O	Patience and cheerful serenity instead of subconscious irritability.	
X	Truthfulness and real feelings instead of vanity and deception.	
E	Goodness and innocence instead of lust and dominant control.	
S	Courage and trust instead of fear and doubt.	
Y	Openness and generosity instead of avarice and greed.	

TOPIC Question 95	**TYPICAL CORE FORMULATIONS** **Of the following formulations, two categories are particularly typical for me:**	1 = very important 2 = second important
T	*"I'm happy to do it!" "What can I do for you?" "That wouldn't have been necessary!" "Shouldn't I rather help you?" "Leave it, I'll do it!" "How can I help you?"*	
F	*"That really hit/wounded me, that hurts me!" "That must always happen to me! "I can't possibly accept that!" "I am completely ecstatic! "I can't live with that!" "That really makes me speechless/ stunned! "I am confused/irritated! "How could she/he ignore me? "That is just incredible!*	
S	*"Yes, but...!" What if...?" "Have we really thought of everything?" "Safe is safe! "You can safely assume that!" "You better take another pair of spare pants with you!" "I have to think about it again!" "I have thought about it once again! "I noticed above all still this! "What would be if?*	
E	*"That's not fair!" "You're not gonna let that happen to you, are you?" "I'm certainly not going to put up with that!" "But I'll clear that up right away" "That's outrageous, there's a sequel!" "I'll sort him out!"*	

Continued question 95 see next page …

... continued question 95:

TOPIC	TYPICAL CORE FORMULATIONS	1 = very important
Question 95	Of the following formulations, two categories are particularly typical for me:	2 = second important
O	"There must be order!" "Without diligence no price!" "Good is not good enough!" "You can do even better!" "Nevertheless..." "It's just not right that...!" "You should...!" "Perfect!" "Exactly!"	
N	"It doesn't matter!" "That's all right!" "No problem!" "I can well understand that!" "Please don't put me under pressure, don't rush me!" "Always one by one" "I am just a little slower!" "Tomorrow is also still another day! "I don't know either!"	
X	"There's no such thing as no such thing!" "We'll get it right again!" "You just have to be calm (stay cool), then it'll work!" "That's no problem at all!" "I (we) can do it" "Don't you just happen to have to ...?" "How would it be if we ...!"	
Z	"It was just a joke!" "Can't you understand a joke?" "Let's...!" "We can really treat ourselves to that!" "Best I buy both! "If already then already! "A little bit of fun must be! "That's a good idea, we'll do that!"	
Y	"Why don't you do it without me?" "Can you just leave me alone?" "Why do you always annoy me?" "Why are you just so hysterical?" "You can explain that quite objectively!	

TOPIC	UNCONSCIOUS, NORMAL & CONSCIOUS ATTITUDE	1 = very important
Question 96	Which two representations of the unconscious, normal and conscious attitude apply most to me?	2 = second important
Y	a) **Unconscious attitude:** isolated, nihilistic, eccentric b) **Normal attitude:** analytical, distant, abstract c) **Conscious attitude:** inventive, wise, energetic	
T	a) **Unconscious attitude:** manipulative, dominant, possessive b) **Normal attitude:** maternal, giving, active c) **Conscious attitude:** caring, friendly, original	
E	a) **Unconscious attitude:** tyrannical, violent, revengeful b) **Normal attitude:** controlling, competing, intense c) **Conscious attitude:** generous, leading, protective	

Continued question 96 see next page ...

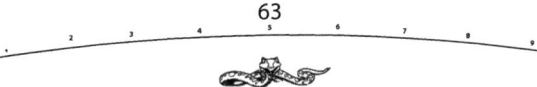

TOPIC	UNCONSCIOUS, NORMAL & CONSCIOUS ATTITUDE	1 = very important
Question 96	**Which two representations of the unconscious, normal and conscious attitude apply most to me?**	2 = second important
S	a) *Unconscious attitude:* dependent, aggressive, cowardly b) *Normal attitude:* dutiful, conscientious, cautious c) *Conscious attitude:* faithful, courageous, trusting	
X	a) *Unconscious attitude:* opportunistic, fraudulent, awkward b) *Normal attitude:* pragmatic, status-conscious, efficient c) *Conscious attitude:* competent, truthful, reliable	
N	a) *Unconscious attitude:* fatalistic, disoriented, stubborn b) *Normal attitude:* adjusted, undecided, indifferent c) *Conscious attitude:* accepting, peaceable, kind	
Z	a) *Unconscious attitude:* excessive, opinionated, bumbling b) *Normal attitude:* active, enjoyable, superficial c) *Conscious attitude:* cheerful, versatile, sober	
F	a) *Unconscious attitude:* snivelling, decadent, in love with death b) *Normal attitude:* aesthetic, romantic, stylish c) *Conscious attitude:* creative, natural, disciplined	
O	a) *Unconscious attitude:* dogmatic, corrosive, supercritical b) *Normal attitude:* perfectionist, thoughtful, critical c) *Conscious attitude:* Critically alert, (cheerfully) relaxed, ethical	

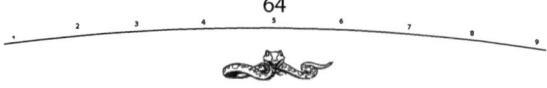

TOPIC	WARNING SIGNS	1 = very important
Question 97	In unconscious, stressful phases of my life I gain the following two impressions (warning signs):	2 = second important
E	I have to put more pressure on my fellow human beings to finally take action.	
T	I believe that I have to inspire others for myself.	
Y	I escape from reality in thoughts, ideas and spiritual worlds.	
N	I believe that I depend on the encouragement of others.	
X	I am increasingly looking for social recognition.	
S	I`m making myself dependent on a leading figure, an authority.	
O	I feel the obligation to do everything myself.	
F	I create drama out of nothing and "enjoy" the strong emotional fluctuations in me.	
Z	Then I think I`ll definitely find something better somewhere else.	

TOPIC	WHAT OTHERS FIND ANNOYING ABOUT ME	1 = very important
Question 98	Two of the following representations, which others find annoying about me, apply to me in a special way:	2 = second important
Z	Selfishness, to sugarcoat everything, in communication always only sending instead of receiving.	
O	(Unspoken) criticism, perfectionism, rigidity.	
Y	Aloof, distant, wanting to be alone, excessive asking and analyzing, difficult to get into emotional contact.	
F	Emotional fluctuations, melancholy, unrealistic expectations.	
X	Superficiality/spuriousness, lack of integrity, success story.	
N	Postponing or avoiding problems/conflicts, lack of clarity.	
T	Excessive helpfulness/interference, manipulation, paternalism.	
S	Mistrust, fears, too much caution and concern, the feeling of being tested.	
E	Control, disrespect, not perceiving truths/interests.	

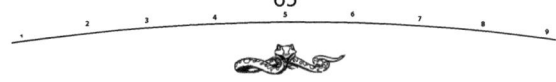

TOPIC	WHY NO RIGHT TO LIVE AND BE LOVED?	1 = very important
Question 99	Why could I have no right to live and be loved deep down in myself?	2 = second important
O	If I'm not perfect, I have no right to live and be loved!	
T	If I am not loving and helpful, I have no right to live and be loved!	
X	If I do not perform, I have no right to live and be loved!	
F	If I am nothing special, I have no right to live and be loved!	
Y	If I do not isolate myself or withdraw, I have no right to live and be loved!	
S	If I do not worry about my safety, I have no right to live and be loved!	
Z	If I am not always optimistic and cheerful, I have no right to live and be loved!	
E	If I am not always strong and control others, I have no right to live and be loved!	
N	If I do not forget myself, I have no right to live and be loved!	

TOPIC	WILLINGNESS TO ACT	1 = very important
Question 100	With the following descriptions regarding my willingness to act I see myself in two points particularly:	2 = second important
E	Active controller (boss) - power-oriented.	
O	Relentless perfectionist - perfection-oriented.	
Z	Enthusiastic visionary (Epicurean) - fun-oriented.	
N	Adapted peacemaker - harmony-oriented.	
T	Considerate helper - love-oriented.	
Y	Quiet specialist (observer) - knowledge-oriented.	
X	Competitive achiever ((dynamic type) - success-oriented.	
S	Loyal skeptic - safety-oriented.	
F	Intensive creative (Romantic) - individuality-oriented.	

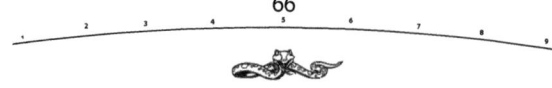

The 27 Subtypes*

HEAD, HEART - OR GUT TYPE

Intrinsic motivation!

(Normal type – Reinforcement type – Countertype)

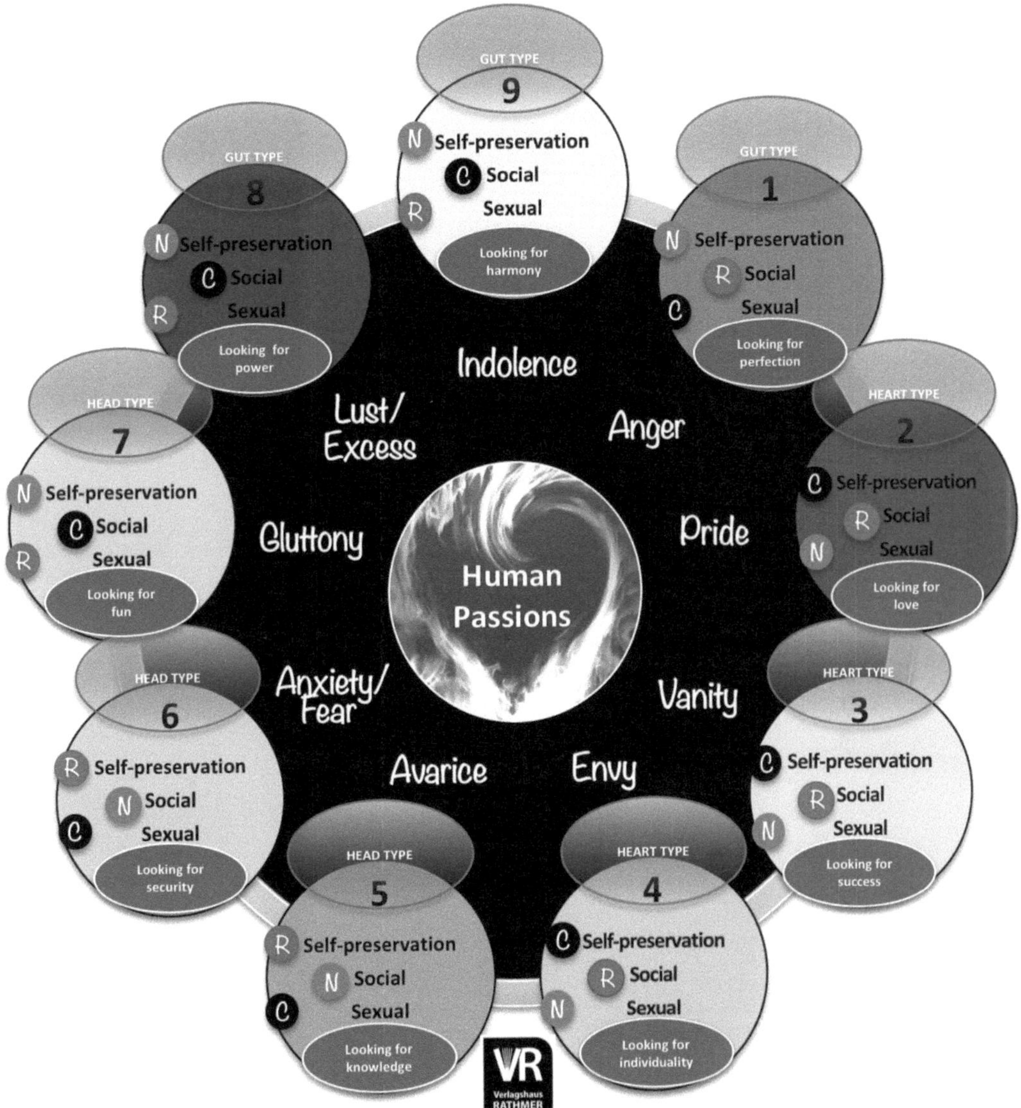

GUT TYPE

9
- N Self-preservation
- C Social
- R Sexual

Looking for harmony

GUT TYPE

8
- N Self-preservation
- C Social
- R Sexual

Looking for power

GUT TYPE

1
- N Self-preservation
- R Social
- C Sexual

Looking for perfection

HEAD TYPE

7
- N Self-preservation
- C Social
- R Sexual

Looking for fun

HEART TYPE

2
- C Self-preservation
- R Social
- N Sexual

Looking for love

Indolence

Lust/ Excess

Anger

Gluttony

Pride

Human Passions

Anxiety/ Fear

Vanity

HEAD TYPE

6
- R Self-preservation
- N Social
- C Sexual

Looking for security

Avarice

Envy

HEART TYPE

3
- C Self-preservation
- R Social
- N Sexual

Looking for success

HEAD TYPE

5
- R Self-preservation
- N Social
- C Sexual

Looking for knowledge

HEART TYPE

4
- C Self-preservation
- R Social
- N Sexual

Looking for individuality

VR Verlagshaus RATHMER

* In the three subtypes of each Enneagram fixation, we distinguish a so-called **normal type**, which lives out its type-specific passion in a "normal" way, a so-called **reinforcement type** that lives its corresponding passion in a "reinforced" way and a so-called **countertype** that negates his respective passion, so as far as possible does not live and avoids it. The **normal type** and the **reinforcement type** are usually the most obvious, but the **countertype** is often not so easy to recognize because its passion is not lived outwardly.

Illness (Disease) Behavior & Polarities

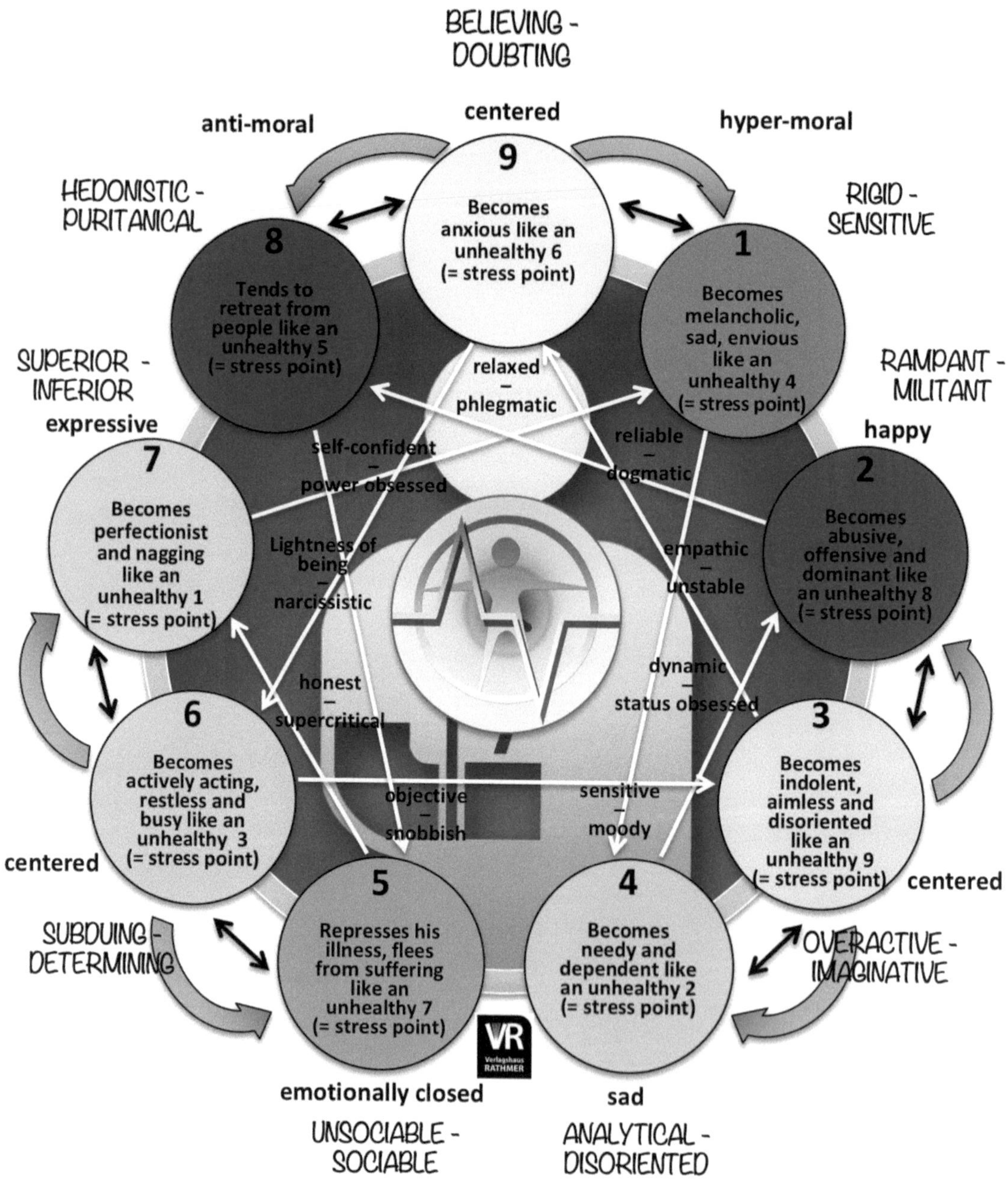

BELIEVING – DOUBTING

anti-moral centered hyper-moral

HEDONISTIC – PURITANICAL

RIGID – SENSITIVE

9 Becomes anxious like an unhealthy 6 (= stress point)

8 Tends to retreat from people like an unhealthy 5 (= stress point)

1 Becomes melancholic, sad, envious like an unhealthy 4 (= stress point)

SUPERIOR – INFERIOR
expressive

RAMPANT – MILITANT
happy

relaxed – phlegmatic

reliable – dogmatic

self-confident – power obsessed

7 Becomes perfectionist and nagging like an unhealthy 1 (= stress point)

Lightness of being – narcissistic

empathic – unstable

2 Becomes abusive, offensive and dominant like an unhealthy 8 (= stress point)

honest – supercritical

dynamic – status obsessed

6 Becomes actively acting, restless and busy like an unhealthy 3 (= stress point)

objective – snobbish

sensitive – moody

3 Becomes indolent, aimless and disoriented like an unhealthy 9 (= stress point)

centered

centered

SUBDUING – DETERMINING

5 Represses his illness, flees from suffering like an unhealthy 7 (= stress point)

4 Becomes needy and dependent like an unhealthy 2 (= stress point)

OVERACTIVE – IMAGINATIVE

emotionally closed

sad

UNSOCIABLE – SOCIABLE

ANALYTICAL – DISORIENTED

VR Verlagshaus RATHMER

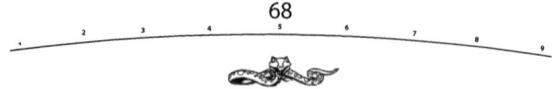

7. Evaluation of the Motivational Enneagram Type (test result)

O = Enneatype 1	F = Enneatype 4	Z = Enneatype 7
T = Enneatype 2	Y = Enneatype 5	E = Enneatype 8
X = Enneatype 3	S = Enneatype 6	N = Enneatype 9

Evaluation table (Date _____/test result type [＿＿])

Please count the letters according to importance:	Number of letters		1 st place result (multiplied by **6**)	2nd place result (multiplied by **3**)
	1 = very important	2 = second important		
How many times „O" (type 1):				
How many times „T " (type 2):				
How many times „X" (type 3):				
How many times „F " (type 4):				
How many times „Y" (type 5):				
How many times „S" (type 6):				
How many times „Z" (type 7):				
How many times „E" (type 8):				
How many times „N" (type 9):				

CONGRATULATION - YOU MADE IT! Now that your work is done, you can evaluate your **Enneagram Test** using the table above to get the desired test result. Please enter the **number of letters** that you marked in the test with **1 = very important**, after the count in the left column (under **number of letters**) under the respective letters **O - T - X - F - Y - S - Z - E - N** gradually into the **evaluation table.** The same thing should be repeated with the number of letters you marked second in the test with **2 = second important**, after you have counted this number before. Then multiply the highest result (the highest letter value) of the left column *(1 = very important)* by the number **6**, multiply the result from the second column *(2 = second important)* by the number **3**. Then you enter the result of your multiplication in the appropriate fields of the table *(1st place result and 2nd place result).* Provided that you have answered the questions to the best of your knowledge and belief with the greatest possible awareness, the test result with the **highest multiplication value** will most likely correspond to your **correct enneatype**, but the result with the **second highest multiplication value** could also be your enneatype, depending on the difference to the highest value in the test evaluation. In any case, by answering the questions you have already learned a lot about what is really important in the **Enneagram** or **type determination**, namely the **basic motivation** of the person to be determined. In this respect the **motivation** determines - even if it is regularly **not lived consciously**, not only the entire **patterns of action and behavior** of a person, but really his **whole life** *with his relationships, his conflicts, his way of being in order to face life in the best possible way.* I wish you *from the bottom of my heart*, that with the help of this test and, if necessary, further literature and living experiences in the field of the enneagram you can clearly recognize which enneatype you are, i.e. **who you really are** and **what constantly drives or motivates you** in the depth of your being.

So that you can evaluate the test even more frequently than just once, there are **two further evaluation tables** printed below:

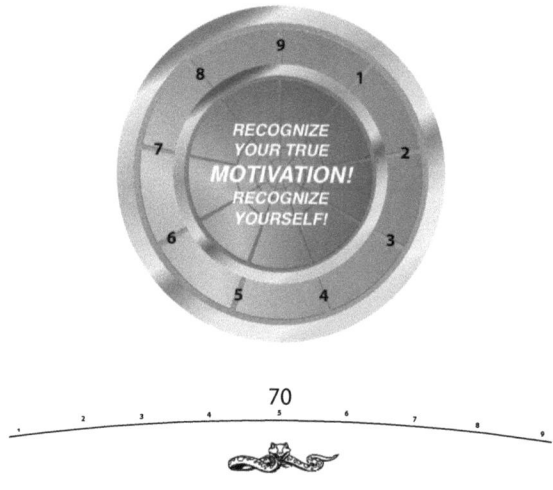

Evaluation table (Date _____/test result type ☐)

Please count the letters according to importance:	Number of letters		1 st place result (multiplied by **6**)	2nd place result (multiplied by **3**)
	1 = very important	2 = second important		
How many times „O" (type 1):				
How many times „T " (type 2):				
How many times „X" (type 3):				
How many times „F " (type 4):				
How many times „Y" (type 5):				
How many times „S" (type 6):				
How many times „Z" (type 7):				
How many times „E" (type 8):				
How many times „N" (type 9):				

Evaluation table (Date _____/test result type ☐)

Please count the letters according to importance:	Number of letters		1 st place result (multiplied by **6**)	2nd place result (multiplied by **3**)
	1 = very important	2 = second important		
How many times „O" (type 1):				
How many times „T " (type 2):				
How many times „X" (type 3):				
How many times „F " (type 4):				
How many times „Y" (type 5):				
How many times „S" (type 6):				
How many times „Z" (type 7):				
How many times „E" (type 8):				
How many times „N" (type 9):				

The 9 Enneatypes, their True Transformation (3.) and their Specific Homeopathic Remedy (4.)

Note: The proper intake of the most suitable **homeopathic remedy** (4) in the correct dosage helps enormously with the enneagrammatic transformation (3), i.e. **patience** instead of **anger** in **type 1**, **love** instead of **pride** in **type 2**, **truthfulness** instead of **vanity** in **type 3**, **authenticity** instead **envy** with **type 4**, **openness** instead of **avarice** with **type 5**, **courage** instead of **fear** with **type 6**, **sobriety** instead of **gluttony** with **type 7**, **goodness** instead of **lust** with **type 8** as well **responsibility** instead of **inertia** with **type 9**.

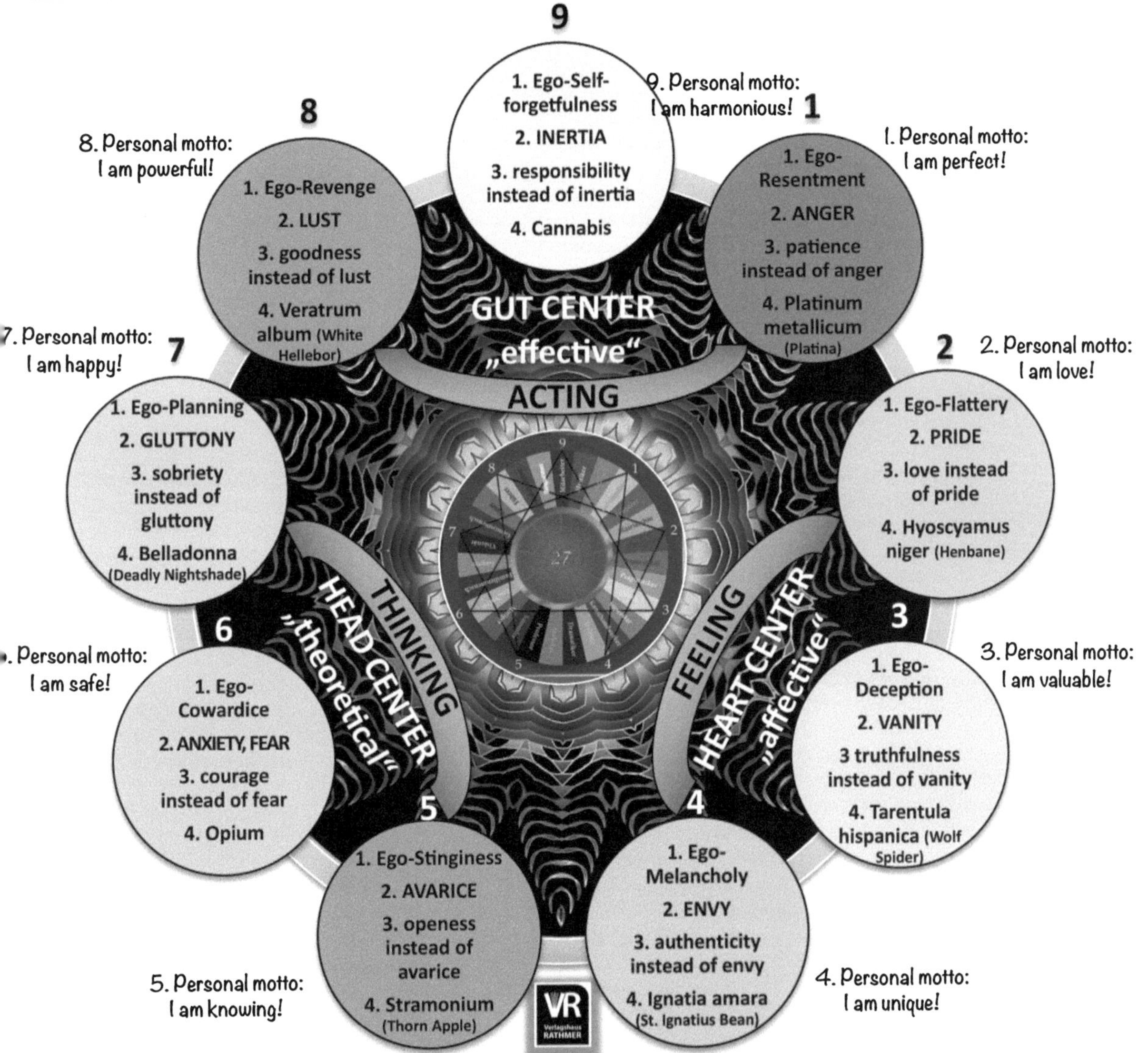

9

1. Ego-Self-forgetfulness
2. INERTIA
3. responsibility instead of inertia
4. Cannabis

9. Personal motto: I am harmonious!

1

1. Ego-Resentment
2. ANGER
3. patience instead of anger
4. Platinum metallicum (Platina)

1. Personal motto: I am perfect!

8

8. Personal motto: I am powerful!

1. Ego-Revenge
2. LUST
3. goodness instead of lust
4. Veratrum album (White Hellebor)

2

2. Personal motto: I am love!

1. Ego-Flattery
2. PRIDE
3. love instead of pride
4. Hyoscyamus niger (Henbane)

7

7. Personal motto: I am happy!

1. Ego-Planning
2. GLUTTONY
3. sobriety instead of gluttony
4. Belladonna (Deadly Nightshade)

3

3. Personal motto: I am valuable!

1. Ego-Deception
2. VANITY
3 truthfulness instead of vanity
4. Tarentula hispanica (Wolf Spider)

6

6. Personal motto: I am safe!

1. Ego-Cowardice
2. ANXIETY, FEAR
3. courage instead of fear
4. Opium

4

4. Personal motto: I am unique!

1. Ego-Melancholy
2. ENVY
3. authenticity instead of envy
4. Ignatia amara (St. Ignatius Bean)

5

5. Personal motto: I am knowing!

1. Ego-Stinginess
2. AVARICE
3. openess instead of avarice
4. Stramonium (Thorn Apple)

GUT CENTER "effective"
ACTING

HEART CENTER "affective"
FEELING

HEAD CENTER "theoretical"
THINKING

VR Verlagshaus RATHMER

In the inner circle: The three intelligence centers HEAD (types 5, 6, 7), HEART (types 2, 3, 4) & GUT (types 8, 9, 1):
Is the focus in your life in **thinking, feeling** or **acting**, so you are a **head, heart** or **gut type**? This question can only be answered in the context of the particular PASSION of the type of Enneagram (1. anger, 2. pride, 3. vanity, 4. envy, 5. avarice, 6. anxiety/fear, 7. gluttony, 8. lust, 9. inertia) and the corresponding INTRINSIC MOTIVATION (1st Perfection, 2nd Love, 3rd Success, 4th Individuality, 5th Knowledge, 6th Safety, 7th Joy of Life, 8th Power, 9th Harmony).

9. Further and supplementary literature by the author from the Publishing House Rathmer

- *Wall calendar* A4 portrait in English: *"The Eternal Enneagram Calendar"*, matt, 21 x 30 cm; spiral binding with hanger, artistic design: Detlef Rathmer, publishing house Rathmer, April 2019
- **Enneagramm-Homöopathie - *Heilung auf der tiefsten Ebene des Menschseins/Krankseins*** Grundlagenband zur Enneagramm-Homöopathie, Band 1, 136 Seiten, broschiertes Taschenbuch, Verlagshaus Rathmer, Billerbeck, 1. Auflage Mai 2019
- **Enneagramm-Homöopathie Band 2 - *Heilung auf der tiefsten Ebene des Menschseins/Krankseins*** Ganzheitliche Heilung nach der Enneagramm-Homöopathie, Band 2, 152 Seiten, broschiertes Taschenbuch, Verlagshaus Rathmer, Billerbeck, 1. Auflage Mai 2019
- **Wer du wirklich bist - *Enneagramm-Wissen in farbigen Schaubildern*** (Mit Enneagramm-Diagnose-Test), 300 Seiten, Taschenbuch, broschiert, Verlagshaus Rathmer, Billerbeck, März 2015
- **Die 27 Persönlichkeiten des Enneagramms - *Erkenne deinen Persönlichkeitstyp im Spiegel des Enneagramms!*** (27 Charakterprofile als Ausdruck der menschlichen Natur), 88 Seiten, broschiertes Taschenbuch, E-Book, Verlagshaus Rathmer, Billerbeck, 2. Auflage, August 2018
- **Rathmer`s Enneagramm-Typentest - *Kompakter Persönlichkeitstest zur Bestimmung des eigenen Enneagrammtyps (Enneatyps/Untertyps/Trityps)*** 52 Seiten, broschiertes Taschenbuch, E-Book, Verlagshaus Rathmer, Billerbeck, Dezember 2017
- **Die Praxis der Typbestimmung** (Sämtliche 36 Typen-Vergleiche zur präzisen und zuverlässigen Bestimmung des Enneagrammtyps unter Berücksichtigung der 27 Untertypen des Enneagramms), 168 Seiten, wahlweise gebundene Ausgabe mit Lesebändchen oder broschiertes Taschenbuch oder E-Book, Verlagshaus Rathmer, Billerbeck, September 2018
- **Rathmer`s großes Enneagramm-Lexikon von A-Z** (Ein Nachschlagewerk über die 9 Enneatypen inklusive der 27 Untertypen und der 27 Tritypen), 356 Seiten, wahlweise gebundene Ausgabe mit Lesebändchen oder broschiertes Taschenbuch oder E-Book, Verlagshaus Rathmer, Billerbeck, Mai 2017
- **Die ewige Suche nach Vollkommenheit, Liebe, Erfolg, Individualität, Wissen, Sicherheit, Lebensfreude, Macht, Harmonie** - Enneagramm-Kalenderreihe: Für jeden Enneagrammtyp einen speziellen sog. ewigen Kalender, der zeitlos schön jeden Monat die wichtigsten Themen ästhetisch und tiefgründig in lebendigen Bildern darstellt, denn ein Bild sagt mehr als tausend Worte, 12 stimmungsvolle Kalenderseiten & eindrucksvolles Deckblatt, A4-Querformat, matt, 21 x 30 cm, Spiralbindung mit Aufhänger, künstlerische Gestaltung: Detlef Rathmer, Verlagshaus Rathmer, April 2019
- **Die weltweit erste Enneagramm-Wandkalender (auch in englischer Sprache)/Tischkalender/Küchenkalender** - Enneagramm-Kalenderreihe: 13 universelle Enneagrammthemen werden hier ästhetisch anspruchsvoll, lehrreich und ausdrucksstark dargestellt, 12 lehrreiche Kalenderseiten & eindrucksvolles Deckblatt, welche die wichtigsten Prinzipien des Enneagramms übersichtlich darstellen, verschiedene Formate: 1. Wandkalender A4-Hochformat, matt, 21 x 30 cm 2. Wandkalender A3-Hochformat, matt, 42 x 30 cm 3. Tischkalender quadratisches Format, matt, 14 x 14 cm 4. Küchenkalender A4-Hochformat, matt, 13 x 30 cm 5. Wandkalender A4-Hochformat in englischer Sprache: „The Eternal Enneagram Calendar", matt, 21 x 30 cm; Spiralbindung mit Aufhänger, künstlerische Gestaltung: Detlef Rathmer, Verlagshaus Rathmer, April 2019
- **Der ewige Kalender der Naturwunder** - Spektakuläre, stimmungsvoll grandiose Naturaufnahmen, die auf einzigartige Weise die Schönheiten der Natur unseres Planeten imposant in einer ästhetisch formvollendeten Weise mit darstellen, qualitativ hochwertiges Druckverfahren, ein immerwährender Wandkalender, 21 x 30 cm, matt, Spiralbindung mit Aufhänger, künstlerische Gestaltung: Detlef Rathmer, Verlagshaus Rathmer, März 2019
- **Der ewige Kalender der Liebe** - Stilvoll und ausdrucksstark, abwechslungsreich auf die Jahreszeiten abgestimmt enthält dieser „Liebes-Kalender" jahrtausendealte Weisheiten um das große Thema der menschlichen Liebe mit eindrucksvollen Fotografien, ein wunderschönes Geschenk für einen geliebten Menschen, einen anderen oder sich selbst, qualitativ hochwertiges Druckverfahren, immerwährender Wandkalender, 21 x 30 cm, matt, Spiralbindung mit Aufhänger, künstlerische Gestaltung: Detlef Rathmer, Verlagshaus Rathmer, März 2019
- **Der ewige Kalender der Selbsterkenntnis** - Jahrtausendealte zeitlose Lebensweisheiten in gelungener Komposition mit dazu passenden stimmungsvollen Fotografien, die täglich zu tiefgreifender Selbsterkenntnis führen, qualitativ hochwertiges Druckverfahren, immerwährender Wandkalender, 21 x 30 cm, matt, Spiralbindung mit Aufhänger, künstlerische Gestaltung: Detlef Rathmer, Verlagshaus Rathmer, April 2019

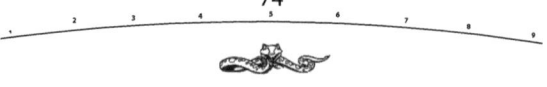

- **7 Wege zu dir selbst** - *Lebenskunst für den Alltag*, 115 Seiten, Taschenbuch, broschiert, Mankau-Verlag, Murnau a. Staffelsee, November 2008
- **Sei still und wisse - Ich bin GOTT!** - *Finde die heilsame Stille in Dir*, 76 Seiten, Taschenbuch, broschiert, Verlagshaus Rathmer, Billerbeck, Juli 2009
- **Rathmer`s Repertorium** - *Das große Repertorium der Geist-/Gemütsrubriken und deren Bedeutung in der Homöopathie*, 1568 Seiten, gebunden, Ledereinband, 5 Lesebändchen, Verlagshaus Rathmer, Billerbeck, Mai 2011 (auch als EBook Edition lizenziert im pdf-Format erhältlich)
- **Das große Enneagramm-Homöopathie Repertorium von A-Z** - *Eine facettenreiche Darstellung der Enneagramm-Homöopathie in Form von Gemüts-, Symbol- und Themenrubriken*, 392 Seiten, gebunden, 1 Lesebändchen, Verlagshaus Rathmer, Billerbeck, Oktober 2014 (auch als EBook Edition lizenziert im pdf-Format erhältlich)
- **Repertorium der hervorstechenden Gemütsrubriken** - *Differenzierung der 9 Enneagramm-Heilmittel in der Homöopathie*, 256 Seiten, gebunden, 1 Lesebändchen, Verlagshaus Rathmer, Billerbeck, September 2014 (auch als EBook Edition lizenziert im pdf-Format erhältlich)
- **Die Dynamik der 9 Enneagramm-Heilmittel** - *Die dynamischen Beziehungen zwischen den einzelnen Heilmitteln der Enneagramm-Homöopathie*, 280 Seiten, gebunden, 1 Lesebändchen, Verlagshaus Rathmer, Billerbeck, Oktober 2014 (auch als EBook Edition lizenziert im pdf-Format erhältlich)
- **Lehrbuch der Enneagramm-Homöopathie** in drei Bänden: **Band 1: Arzneimittellehre Typen I - IV**, 348 Seiten, Taschenbuch, broschiert, Verlagshaus Rathmer, Billerbeck, Februar 2013 (auch als EBook Edition lizenziert im pdf-Format erhältlich) **Band 2: Arzneimittellehre Typen V - IX**, 420 Seiten, Taschenbuch, broschiert, Verlagshaus Rathmer, Billerbeck, Februar 2013 (auch als EBook Edition lizenziert im pdf-Format erhältlich), **Band 3: Enneagramm-Homöopathie Repertorium**, 376 Seiten, Taschenbuch, broschiert, Verlagshaus Rathmer, Billerbeck, Februar 2013 (auch als EBook Edition lizenziert im pdf-Format erhältlich)
- **Der Kern der Heilmittel** - *Die zentralen Geist-/Gemütsrubriken der homöopathischen Arzneimittel/The central mind rubrics of the homoeopathic medicines*, homöopathische Arzneimittellehre, zweisprachig deutsch/englisch, 526 Seiten, gebunden, 1 Lesebändchen, Verlagshaus Rathmer, Billerbeck, Dezember 2011 (auch als EBook Edition lizenziert im pdf-Format erhältlich)
- **Homöopathische Arzneimittellehre der Single-Rubriken aus dem Geist-/Gemütsbereich** - *Das geistige Wesen der 500 wichtigsten Heilmittel in der Homöopathie*, 348 Seiten, Taschenbuch, broschiert, Verlagshaus Rathmer, Billerbeck, Juli 2009
- **Fallanalyse in der Homöopathie nach Sehgal** - *Autodidaktisches Lern- und Arbeitsbuch anhand von 36 Fällen aus der homöopathischen Praxis*, 320 Seiten, Taschenbuch, broschiert, Eva-Lang-Verlag, Worpswede, März 2008
- **Enneagramm-Homöopathie - Unterrichtsmaterial** - *20 Unterrichtseinheiten für das Selbststudium der Enneagramm-Homöopathie*, 376 Seiten, EBook Edition im pdf-Format, Verlagshaus Rathmer, 2016 (lfd. aktualisiert)
- **Das Unterrichtsskript zur Sehgal-Ausbildung** - *Unterrichtsmaterialien aus der Sehgal-Schule für das Eigenstudium der Sehgal-Methode*, 500 Seiten, EBook im pdf-Format, Verlagshaus Rathmer, 2012 (lfd. aktualisiert)
- **Gesetzeskunde für Heilpraktiker** *zur Vorbereitung auf die amtsärztliche Überprüfung beim Gesundheitsamt*, 208 Seiten, EBook Edition im pdf-Format, Verlagshaus Rathmer, August 2015.

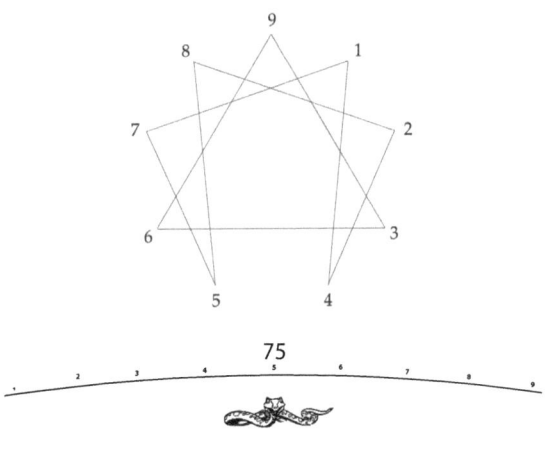

10. Additional YouTube videos in German by the author (296 videos, July 2019)

- **Gemeinsamkeiten & Unterschiede der Enneagrammtypen - 36-teilige Lernvideo-Reihe** *(Differenzierende Betrachtungen sämtlicher 36 Vergleichskombinationen der 9 Enneagrammtypen, begleitend und vertiefend dazu dient das kompakte Typbestimmungsbuch "**Die Praxis der Typbestimmung**")*

- **Enneagramm in 3 Minuten - Lernvideos** *(In nur 3 Minuten plus max. 59 Sekunden erklärt Enneagramm-Experte und Heilpraktiker Detlef Rathmer ein zentrales Lebensthema aller 9 Enneatypen anhand eines ausgewählten Schaubildes aus seinem Buch "**Wer du wirklich bist - Enneagramm-Wissen in farbigen Schaubildern**" oder eines Schaubildes aus seinem Unterricht)*

- **Die 27 Untertypen des Enneagramms - 27-teilige Lernvideo-Reihe** *(Enneagramm-Experte und Heilpraktiker Detlef Rathmer erklärt kurz und prägnant das Grundthema der jeweiligen 27 Untertypen anhand eines Schaubildes aus seinem Enneagramm-Unterricht oder seiner Enneagramm-Bücher, begleitend und vertiefend dazu dient das Buch "**Die 27 Persönlichkeiten des Enneagramms - 27 Charakterprofile als Ausdruck der menschlichen Natur - Erkenne deinen Persönlichkeitstyp im Spiegel des Enneagramms!**")*

- **Enneagramm - Weiterentwicklung & Transformation - Lernvideo-Reihe** *(Hier werden notwendige und hilfreiche Entwicklungsschritte und -möglichkeiten der einzelnen 9 Enneagrammtypen anschaulich dargestellt, momentan noch im fortlaufenden Aufbau)*

- **Enneagramm-Homöopathie - mehrteilige Videoreihe** *(Hier werden interessante Themen rund um das Enneagramm, die Homöopathie und die Enneagramm-Homöopathie dargestellt, wird regelmäßig erweitert)*

- **Tip:** *Subscribe to the Youtube channel by Detlef Rathmer so you will not miss a future video!*

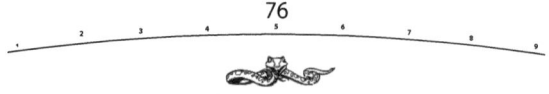